MW01258422

Pattern Weaving
Basics for the Handloom

0 11557 00053 5

Pattern Weaving

Basics for the Handloom

Rabbit Goody

Photography by Richard Walker

STACKPOLE
BOOKS

Copyright ©2012 by Stackpole Books

Published by
STACKPOLE BOOKS
5067 Ritter Road
Mechanicsburg, PA 17055
www.stackpolebooks.com

Printed in the United States of America

10 9 8 7 6 5 4 3 2 1

FIRST EDITION

Cover design by Wendy Reynolds
Cover photo by Richard Walker

Library of Congress Cataloging-in-Publication Data

Goody, Rabbit.
 Pattern weaving : basics for the handloom / Rabbit Goody ; photography by Richard Walker. — First Edition.
 pages   cm   ISBN 978-0-8117-0053-5 (pbk.)
1. Hand weaving. 2. Handlooms. I. Title.
TT848.G667 2012
746.42—dc23

2012015836

Contents

Introduction

In its most elementary form, weaving is a binary process that involves the crossing of vertical or lengthwise yarns, the *warp* thread, with horizontal or widthwise yarns, the *filling*, or *weft* threads. The horizontal yarns go either over or under the vertical yarns in a set pattern or sequence that generates a design. The tool used to produce the woven object is the *loom*, operated by the weaver.

How is weaving different from knitting or other fabric construction? Weaving creates fabric that can be easily cut and sewn. It is also an efficient way to produce multiples—several scarves, blankets, placemats, and so on.

With weaving, you can make patterns that are an integral part of the cloth, not simply something printed on the surface. And weaving is highly versatile from a design standpoint: You can make patterns with color but also with weave structure, or with combinations of both.

This book on basic pattern weaving will teach you all the steps you need to weave on a foot-treadle handloom. The tips and variations will help you to explore your own creative weaving ideas and give you a firm understanding of the whys and hows of handweaving. It is set up to familiarize you with common patterns and weave structures, but it is not strictly a cookbook of designs.

There are four projects in this book with complete directions, but when you finish it, you will understand how to use the weave structures and techniques from each of these projects to make a wide variety of other items and to explore your own ideas in pattern weaving.

I don't have a clear understanding of why I began weaving, but I know that I have a natural affinity for it. I somehow understood weaving before I ever began to weave. I was part of the hippie generation and the back-to-the-land movement of the 1960s and '70s, and I wanted to build my own house, grow my own food, and make my own clothing. (I have, in fact, done all that.) But I began making my clothing by spinning, using a drop spindle made from a stick and a potato. When I started weaving, I understood how weaving worked in the same way that someone who picks up a musical instrument can just simply play that instrument without being formally taught. I think of weaving and my relationship to it as a part of the human consciousness. Making cloth is innately human. In addition to food and shelter, every culture makes some form of clothing.

I have been working as a professional weaver for more than thirty-five years, both as an independent trade crafter and as a museum interpreter and curator. As a professional weaver in the 1970s, making a living by my craft, I was sure that there were better ways to efficiently weave cloth than the methods that were being taught by revival handweavers to each other. What seemed to be missing was an efficiency and a complexity of production that existed in the seventeenth and eighteenth centuries, when handweaving was the only way that fabrics were produced.

I was fortunate that I worked in the historical museum field and had access to collections of rare books and tools that allowed me to understand the technology of French, German, and English weavers from the sixteenth century forward. What I realized was that much of the historical weavers' information had been incorporated into the textile trades and the textile industry, but it was ultimately lost to the modern handweaver.

Today handweaving has become an art form as well as a trade. I stand with a foot in two worlds: one in the world of the handweaver producing beautiful and useful textiles and one in the world of the trade weaver running a craft shop in much the same way that weavers in the late eighteenth and early nineteenth centuries did.

I weave on many types of handlooms and power looms. Some of our equipment is old and recycled power looms that were run on flat belts from stationary engines. Our more modern mechanical jacquard from the 1960s originally was making fabrics for automobiles. I weave on barn-frame looms and on a Weavebird (LeClerc) computer-controlled handloom.

Much of my weaving work is the reproduction of textiles from the past, but my interest is also in how textiles were produced using the equipment of earlier time periods. My focus then is in process and methods.

The goal of this book is to teach methods of production and the process of basic pattern weaving that will allow readers to create whatever textiles they want with the efficiency and quality that empowers them.

The Loom and Other Pattern-Weaving Tools

Four-Harness Foot-Treadle Loom

This book uses a four-harness jack loom, but it does not matter what loom you are using. The basics of weaving on a foot-treadle harness loom are the same. There are three basic types of looms, all characterized by the movement of the harnesses, also called shafts. There is one kind in which the harnesses are raised when you step on a treadle, another kind in which the harnesses are lowered when you step on a treadle, and a third kind in which some harnesses are raised while the others are being lowered. The important function of the harnesses is to make a division between the threads you will send your shuttle over and the threads you will send your shuttle under. It does not matter for basic weaving how that is accom-

plished. All looms have the same basic parts. The photo diagrams on the following pages will help you familiarize yourself with the parts of the loom and their functions.

- Warp beam: The length of the warp is stored here before it is woven.
- Back beam: A cross member on the loom that the warp goes over to run in a flat plane to the harnesses and beater.
- Brake: Used to keep the tension on the warp.
- Castle: The top of the loom that houses the harnesses.
- Harnesses: Frames that move up and down and hold the eyelets, called heddles, through which the warp threads pass to create the patterns.
- Heddles: Eyelets through which the individual warp threads are threaded.
- Treadles: The foot pedals that move the harnesses up or down.
- Lamms: Cross pieces that allow connections between the harnesses and the treadles so that you can make combinations of harnesses. Not all treadle looms have lamms.
- Breast Beam: The cross piece that the web goes over at the front of the loom.
- Cloth Beam: The roller where the woven web is stored during weaving. The ratchet and pawl on the cloth beam keeps the tension on the cloth and allows it to be wound up during the weaving process.
- Reed: Maintains the density of the warp threads and also is used to pack the filling yarns into place during the weaving process. It sits in a groove in the beater and is held in place by the beater cap. Reeds come in many different densities. You should have 8-, 10-, 12-, and 15-dent reeds (indicating the number of openings per inch in the reed). But you can sley many combinations to achieve different densities using a single reed. Reeds should be the width of your loom.

beater

lamms

Loom Parts

castle

harnesses

2 **3** **4**

1

beater cap

back beam

breast beam

reed

race

cloth beam

warp beam

beater

handle for cloth beam ratchet

brake

treadles

brake pedal

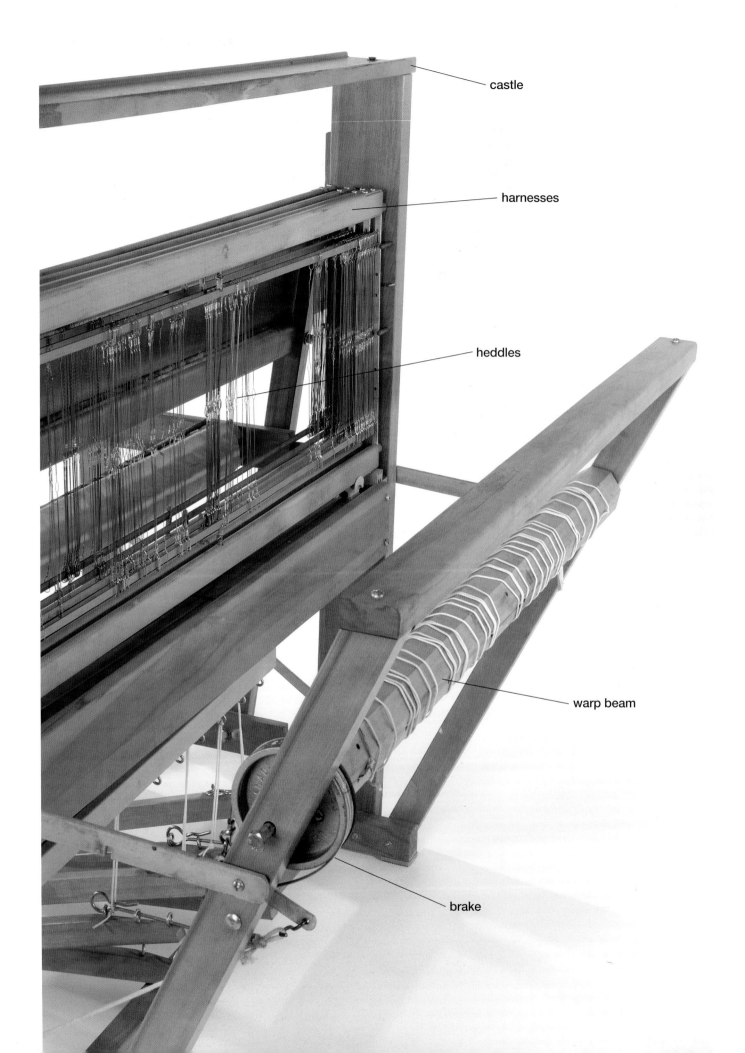

castle

harnesses

heddles

warp beam

brake

Warping Board or Warping Reel

Warping boards come in different sizes and are commonly a yard from side to side. Most warping boards can be hung against a wall at a height that is comfortable for you to wind your warp. Warps are wound horizontally across, going from the top to the bottom and back to the top following the same path. The number of times you go across will depend on the width of your board and the length of your warp.

Warping reels are vertical measuring devices that allow you to stand and turn the reel as you wind the warp. The distances between the vertical uprights are usually in increments of ½ yard or 1 yard. Most warping reels can be folded up and stored out of the way when not in use. In this book, I use a warping reel rather than a warping board.

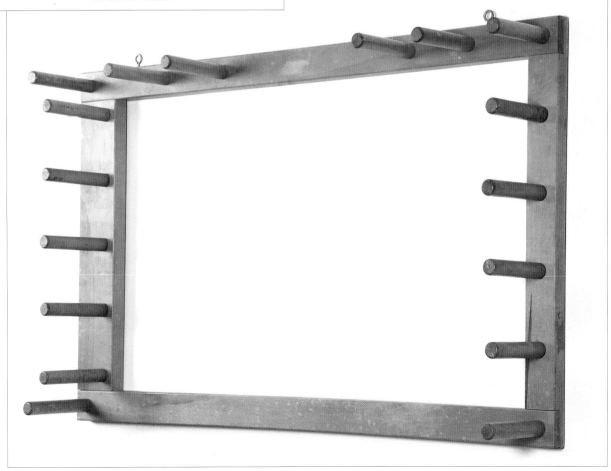

raddle

Raddle

A raddle, or spreader, is a temporary piece with divisions that is used to spread the warp out to its full width during the beaming-on process. It can be made from a board with nails at every inch or half inch. Leclerc Loom Company makes a raddle that fits into the beater where the reed usually sits.

Shuttle

There are two basic types of shuttles that handweavers use for pattern weaving. The most common is a side-delivery, or boat, shuttle. The other is an end-delivery, or fly, shuttle, which is used when weaving wide widths or widths that are at least twice as wide as the length of the shuttle. In this book we will be using only side-delivery shuttles, because most of our weaving widths will be narrow.

A side-delivery shuttle carries a hollow bobbin that fits onto a harness in the center of the shuttle. The filling yarn is wound on the bobbin in a separate step and placed into the shuttle. There is a hole or slot on the side of the shuttle through which the yarn passes. This slot or hole is called a *fare lead*. The yarn unwinds through the side of the shuttle, hence the name side-delivery shuttle. The bobbin spins as it unwinds in a side-delivery shuttle.

There are many different shuttles on the market. The Schacht boat shuttles are very well designed, and the plastic bobbins Schacht produces fit the shuttles well.

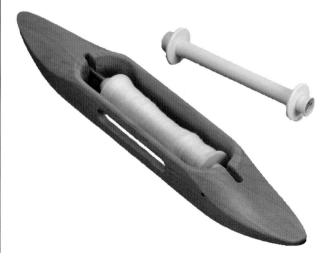

Bobbins, Pirns, and Quills

These are used for holding the filling or weft yarn. They are placed inside a shuttle and sent across the warp. Schacht makes excellent bobbins.

Bobbin Winders

Winders are used to rotate a bobbin or quill so that you can wind your filling yarn very tightly. There are several bobbin winders on the market. I use a manual winder in this book. An adjustable electric winder works well and can be purchased from weaving suppliers.

Cross Sticks

Cross sticks, also called leash sticks, come in pairs. You will need at least one pair of cross sticks that are wider than the width of your loom. These can be flat, round, or oval. They need to be extremely smooth, and both sticks should be the same size and shape. They should have a hole at each end so they can be tied securely but temporarily together.

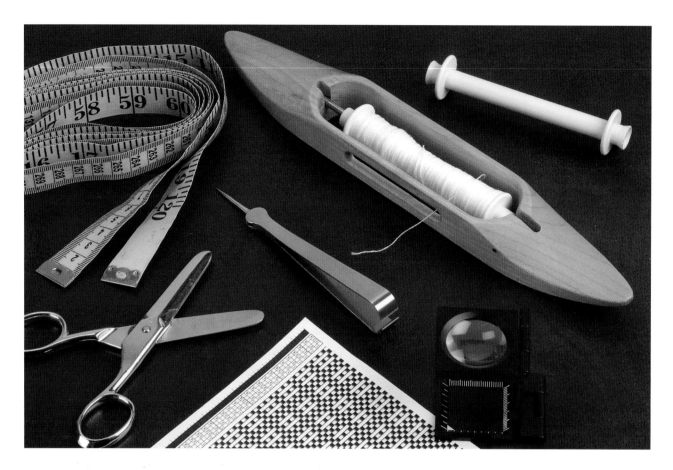

Hooks

There are two basic types of hooks: those used for threading the heddles and those used for sleying the reed. Threading hooks are long and narrow with a small hook at the end. Sleying hooks are usually flat and are often made of brass, copper, or thin wood.

Measuring tapes

Cloth or plastic quilter's tapes of 110 inches are very useful. Have at least two or three tape measures available.

Linen Tester

Also called a pick glass, this is a magnifying glass with a scale for measuring the quality of fabric.

Pins

T pins or large-headed pins will come in handy.

Wooden Ruler and Short Straightedge

Tape measures are handy, but you still need a wooden ruler or short straightedge to wind threads to get end counts and setts.

Scissors

It is helpful to have three types of cutting scissors: a pair of 4-inch blunt-end scissors, a pair of sharp embroidery scissors, and a pair of cloth shears.

Basic Skills

The Warping Process

The warp is the foundation of every weaving project. *Warping* is the measuring of all the lengthwise threads in a piece of cloth. Although a piece of fabric is made of many threads, we refer to the warp as a whole in the singular. You can wind one or many threads at a time to create the warp, and the threads can be of different colors, sizes, and textures. For every warp, however, there are three basic figures needed: length, width, and the number of threads in each inch.

The length is measured by winding the threads on either a warping board or warping reel. For demonstration, I will be using a warping reel.

First take a tape measure and measure out one length of string that will be the same length as your warp. You will put this *guide string* on the warping reel and use it as a guide for winding the warp yarns.

When you begin to wind the warp, you will take a group of threads in hand and wind them down the warping reel to the end of the guide string where you have placed the end peg. You will then loop the yarns around the peg. You will follow the same guide-string path back up the warping reel to the top peg where you started. Then you will loop the warp yarns around the top peg and begin the whole process again. You will not cut the warp when you are winding, because warps are continuous. It doesn't matter which way you loop your warp yarns over the end peg, just be consistent. Make sure you loop the yarns over the peg the same way every time.

The second warp measurement is the total width of the warp in inches. Although the warp is continuous, you will mark off the width in inch increments with *marking strings* so that you don't have to count the total number of threads in a warp. You will wind and count 1 inch at a time and mark it off. These marking strings will later be called *raddle marks*. They are temporary and will be removed in the next step. They are there to help you keep track of how many inches you have wound and for you to double-check when you have finished, so that you can determine whether you have indeed wound the correct width. When you go to the next step, these strings make it easy to spread the warp out to its full width on the loom.

Finally, you need to determine how many threads there will be in each inch of the warp. The number of threads per inch will differ depending on what type of pattern you are weaving. We will discuss this for each project. Because you wind the warp while marking the width off in inch increments, you will need to know the number of threads per inch before you start.

Planning and Preparing a Warp

Let's say you want to weave two scarves that are 10 inches wide and 2½ yards long. So how do you set up a warp to create a scarf that finishes at a certain length and width? You need to make the warp long enough to yield two scarves (5 yards), plus accommodate loom waste, take-up, and the relaxation that occurs when you cut a web off the loom.

The size of a project on the loom is different from the size of a project when it is taken off the loom, because weaving is done under tension. Always remember that there is a change between the dimensions on the loom and off the loom. Usually, whatever you're weaving is somewhat wider and longer on the loom than it is when you take it off the loom.

You will first determine the length of the warp. To figure out the length you will need to know the measurement of your warping reel. Warping reels usually come in yard increments. You will measure a length that will yield two scarves and a sample, so each warp thread must be 6 yards long. That is how long you will make your first warp.

Next you determine the width. You want your scarves to be 10 inches wide, and you know that they will change dimension when you take them off the loom, so you will wind your warp to be 12 inches wide on the loom.

To figure number of threads per inch, you will need a wooden ruler to determine how closely to set your warp yarn. This is called the density or ends per inch (EPI).

Winding a Warp

Warping is the beginning of your cloth, so it's important to pay attention to neatness and consistency during the process. The more neat and consistent your warp is, the better your cloth will be. Here are the tools and materials you will need:

- Warping reel (or warping board)
- Cones of yarn for warp
- Top peg and end peg
- Cross pegs
- Scissors
- Guide string
- Marking string (seine twine works best)
- Contrasting cord for tying your cross
- Plastic bag
- Something for labeling the warp if you are storing it

Before you start, make sure you have plenty of space. You will need a place on the floor where you can set up your cones of yarn and have a clear path to your warping reel. Place the cones so that you can lead yarn from them over the back beam of your loom and then to your warping reel. If you can't position your warping reel near your loom like this, you can use a tension rod stretched in a doorway instead of the back beam. The idea is to unwind your warp yarn from the cones in a smooth and steady way. Pulling the yarn up over some sort of bar—either the back beam of the loom or a curtain rod tensioned in a doorway—will keep the cones from falling over and keep your yarn coming into your hand smooth and straight and at the same tension, whether the cones you're using are big or small. Your goal is to have all your yarns or threads at an even tension and unwinding smoothly and steadily as you create your warp.

Tip: Having more than one cone of a yarn makes winding the warp easier and faster. We will start by using one or two cones to show you the system, but in general you should use at least four ends or cones of yarn if you can.

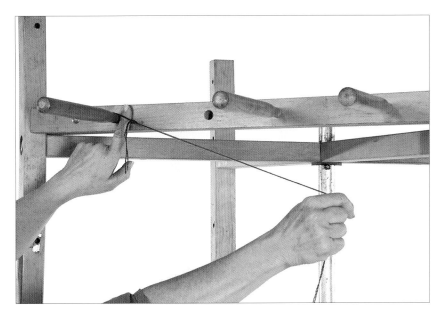

Once you have your cones set up, take the first ends and tie them around the top left-hand peg of the warping reel, leaving a big enough loop to slide your finger through.

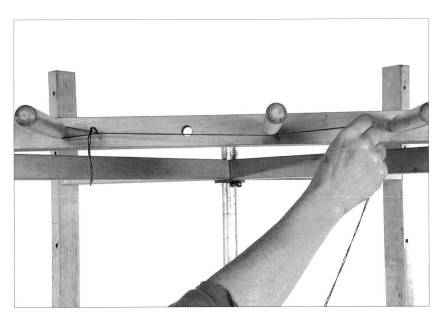

When you wind a warp you need to make a cross. The cross is also called the lease or leash. Its function is to keep track of the order of the threads. To make a cross as you are winding, you need to pick a crossing pattern for making your loops over and under the pegs as you wind your threads down the warping reel and back up again. The pattern I use starts by going under the middle peg.

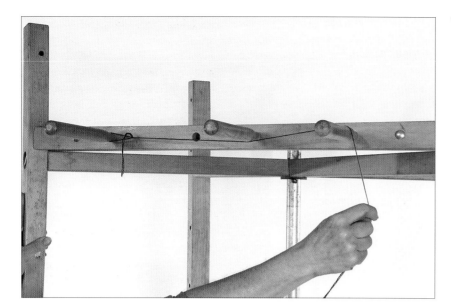

Then go over the third peg.

From the third peg, take the thread over the middle peg, and under the first peg. The warp is continuous so try to keep the tension in your hand even and firm. You do not want the warp yarns to be super tight, but you want to avoid letting any of them go slack. The more neatly and evenly you can make your warp the better.

Each length following the guide string down the warping reel equals the number of threads in your hand and counts as ends in the warp. While holding the yarns in your right hand and moving the reel with your left hand, turn the reel, angling the yarn down gradually, and wind the same number of times around your bottom peg. Follow the same path back up to your cross. If you are holding two threads going down, that's two ends of your warp, and when you come back up the same path you are adding two more threads to the width of your warp. The length never changes once you have established the top and bottom ends of the warp with your guide string and pegs.

The most important thing to remember while you are winding the warp is making the cross and keeping count of the number of threads in each inch. Wind an inch by counting the number of ends in your hand. Go down and then back up the number of times necessary to make 1 inch, and keep winding until you have the correct number of ends to make 1 inch for your project.

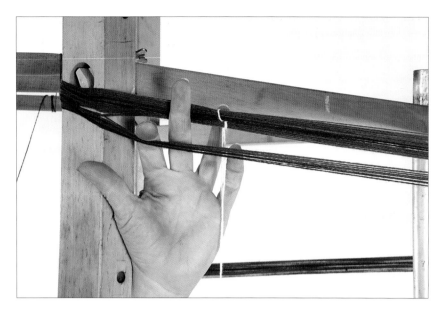

Put in your first raddle mark by tying your marking string around the yarns with a half hitch (the first half of a bow) and leave that marker thread long so it can wrap around the next group of threads.

Continue winding until you have the total number of threads in each inch and the total number of inches you need for the width of your warp.

When you have the correct number of inches, the last threads in your warp need to be cut from the cones. Tie them in a loop around the top peg, again leaving a loop big enough for you to slide your finger in. Tie the yarns to themselves.

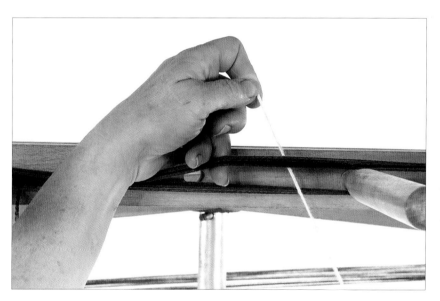

Tying the Cross

The next step is very important because it will preserve the order of your warp threads and help you thread the loom at a later stage. This step is called tying the cross.

Take a double piece of string that is strong and contrasting in color to your warp. Pass it through the right side of the cross from the front of the warping reel to the back.

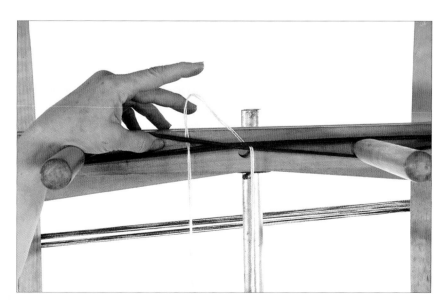

Then bring the string back toward you through the left side of the cross so that the two ends are facing you.

Pull the two ends gently forward and check to see that all of the warp threads are caught in the loop and there are no threads not in the loop.

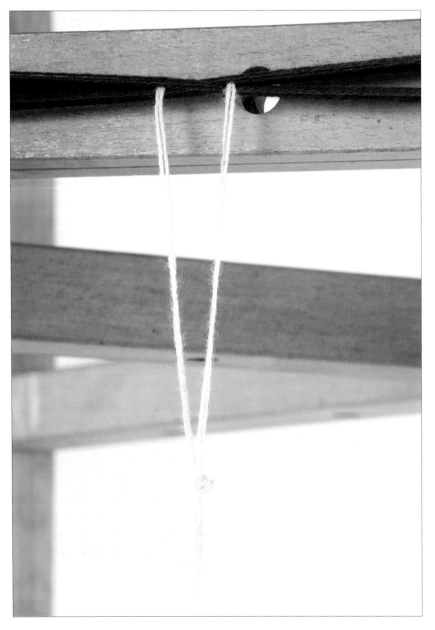

Make an overhand knot at the far end of the string so that you have a long loop.

Do not include the loop from the start of your warp or the end of your warp. This is only a loop around the cross.

You are preserving the cross so that you can transfer it with the warp to the loom. A working loop is large, allowing you to put your fingers or hand through without disturbing the threads that are contained in the loop. The working loops will be very helpful during the steps in which you are putting the warp on the loom.

Next you will put a loop through all of the warp threads at the top, or head end, of the warp. This includes the loops that you made to start and end the warp. Again, tie a working loop that is long and use an over-hand knot.

To take the warp off the reel, cut the loop at the bottom end of the warp. This is where you transform the continuous warp into a group of ends that you can spread onto a beam. Hang onto the warp threads above where you are cutting the end. Don't let them spring back. Grasp the warp with your left hand above the peg and use your right hand to cut all the loops as one group. You can either slip your scissors into the loop around the peg, or on most warping devices, you can pull the peg and cut the loops.

Do not let go of the warp.

With your right hand pick up the plastic bag. Keeping the warp under some tension, slowly coil the warp into the bag.

If you have been using a reel, use your body to turn the reel slowly, letting the warp cascade into the bag.

Don't allow the warp to fall off. Gradually allow it to fall into the bag as you unwind it from the warping reel. Warning: Do not make a chain of the warp. Older weavers and books recommend chaining, but I have found that the resulting twists in the warp make it more difficult to beam the warp under tension. Again, I urge you *not* to make a chain.

Store the warp with the head end hanging out of the top of the bag. Keep it away from the loom until you have prepared the loom to accept the warp. The most important part of the warp is the cross. As long as you have tied the head end, there is nothing that can really go wrong with it.

Loom Preparation and Beaming On

Once the warp is wound and safely in a plastic bag, you will prepare the loom to accept the warp. The area where you store the warp for weaving is called the *warp beam*. When we wind the warp onto the beam for storage, we call it "beaming the warp," or "beaming on." No matter what brand of loom you have, this system will work if you understand the reasons for each step. The goal is to store the warp on the warp beam as evenly as possible, as flat across as possible, and as tightly wound as possible. A good brake on the warp beam is essential. Make sure you understand how the brake on your loom works. At right is a list of the tools and materials you will need.

- A raddle, or spreader, marked off in inches or ½ inches
- Duct tape (the removable kind is best)
- Scissors
- Seine twine
- Tape measure
- Rubber bands (thick ones work best)
- Cross sticks, round or oval, wider than the width of the loom (flat ones aren't nearly as good)
- Apron stick, sturdy and narrower than the warp beam
- 12 to 20 strips of wood, wider than the warp beam, about ½ inch to 1 inch wide

Preparing the Loom

There are some important steps to follow before you take your warp out of the bag.

Clear a path from the front of the loom (left side of photo) to the back of the loom and down to the warp beam.

Take the reed out of the beater. Remove the beater cap, unless you use it to cap your raddle as well. If you do, then just set it in the uppermost position.

Open all the harness hooks that tension the heddles. Move the heddles to the sides of the harnesses so that you have a clear space at least as wide as the piece you will be weaving.

Place the raddle in the beater in place of the reed. If the raddle doesn't fit into the groove for the reed, use duct tape (or, after the next step, tie it in place with the cross slings).

Now you will make and tie cross slings. Take two lengths of seine twine long enough to go from the back beam to the beater doubled. Fold them in half and tie one around the back beam on the right side and one around the back beam on the left side.

Make a cross in each one and tie them around the lower part of the raddle in the beater, holding the beater back against the castle of the loom so that the beater stays in the rearmost position and is held by the cross slings. Make these ties with bows since they are temporary. They should be far enough to the sides of the loom so that you can easily spread your warp to the width that you will be weaving.

Now place two cross sticks halfway across the cross slings. Make sure your cross sticks are longer than the width of your loom. Slide them through one of the cross slings, placing one stick on one side of the cross and the other stick through the other side of the cross.

Place the sticks a finger's distance apart and secure one end of each stick with duct tape, or with string if there are holes in the ends. Take the apron stick from the warp beam and unwind it so that it lies up on the cross slings ready to accept the looped end of the warp.

Before moving on, check to make sure you have done all of the following:

• You have a way to spread the warp, either by ½-inch or 1-inch sections.

• The cross sticks are behind the harnesses ready to accept the cross.

• You have an apron stick ready to accept the warp loop.

• You have a secure way to attach the apron stick to the warp beam.

• You have duct tape or string to secure the ends of the cross sticks and a way to close the top of each section of the raddle, either with rubber bands or the beater cap.

Now you are ready to get your warp out of the bag.

Beaming On

Stand at the front of the loom (left side of photo). Take the head end of the warp out of the bag, leaving the bag on the floor in the weaver's position. Pass the warp over the raddle and through the harnesses to the cross sticks. Try not to let it get caught.

Move to the back of the loom. Pick up the cross by taking the loop and hold it between your hands in the form of a circle.

Take the two outer edges of the
circle and bring them up and then
together. This will fold the circle in
half, bending the two ends up to
meet each other. Pull up slightly and
you now will have the cross exactly
as you made it on the warping reel,
with each part of the cross on one
side of the loop ready for the cross
sticks.

Slide the cross sticks through the
cross, one on each side of the cross.

Put the cross sticks through the cross sling.

Secure the two ends of the sticks together a finger's distance apart with duct tape or string.

If there are holes in the ends of your cross sticks, you can secure them with string rather than duct tape.

apron stick

An apron stick is used to attach the warp to the warp beam. The apron stick should be sturdy enough that it will not bend under the tension of the warp.

Take the apron stick and run it through the beginning loop that you made on the warping reel, then through all of the loops of the warp as a unit, and then through the last loop that you ended the warp with on the warping reel.

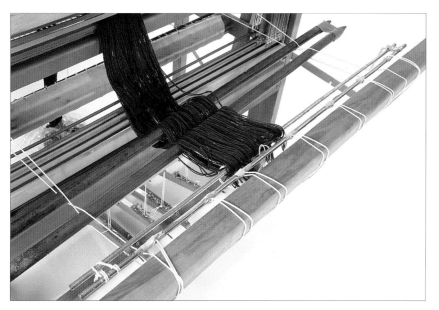

If your loom has a canvas apron on the warp beam or a string system on the warp beam, you will need to attach the apron stick with at least three strings: one string on each end and one in the middle. Use the seine twine and cut three pieces that can be doubled and are the same length.

Use a lark's head knot to attach the apron stick to whatever apron system you have on the loom. If you do not have an apron on your loom, make your strings long enough so that the apron stick can come up over the back beam and within a few inches of the harnesses. This will enable you to weave to the very end of your warp.

Now you will spread the warp in the raddle. Go to the front of the loom. Spread the warp out in the raddle at the full width that it will be woven. The raddle string that we used to mark off each inch while we wound the warp on the reel should be in a position close to where the raddle is located in the beater. Take a tape measure and find the approximate middle of the loom. From the center, measure out to the left and right one-half of the width that the warp will be woven.

Reach in and find the free end of the raddle marker string and undo a 1-inch section. Place it in the open raddle section that corresponds to the width that you have marked.

Continue taking each 1-inch section and placing it in the next slot in the raddle until you have spread the warp out to its full width. The result should look like the bottom photo.

Place rubber bands across the top of the raddle or put the beater cap down so that the groups of 1-inch warp threads cannot be lifted out of their inch slots.

Go to the back of the loom. Cut the cross string that you placed around the cross on the warping reel. Be careful not to cut the warp. Cut the string that you used to tie the loop end of the warp. Spread the loop end of the warp as wide as the warp is spread in the raddle. The warp should look straight from the raddle to the cross to the apron stick.

Be sure you have completed these steps before moving on:

- Secure the apron stick to the warp beam.
- Check the cross and make sure it is secure.
- Check the raddle and make sure groups cannot jump out of the sections.

Now you are ready to wind the warp on the warp beam. At this point, you may want to start working with a helper, if you have one.

Winding on the Warp

The first part of this process is making the warp ready to beam. Divide the warp into two sections, or more if the warp is wide. Hold one section a few feet away from the front of the loom. Shake it up and down under tension as if it were the reins on a horse. Do not run your hands along the warp yarns as this creates loose threads. Hold the section as flat as you can and snap the warp threads from side to side and then "milk" any loose threads down toward your hand—stroke the loose threads into your hand without letting go and without disturbing the rest of the warp. When that section looks smooth and even, put it down gently and go to the next section. Repeat the same process with each section until the warp looks evenly prepared a few feet from the front of the loom.

Once the warp looks smooth, have a helper hold all of the warp threads in two sections, one in each hand, with as much tension on the threads as possible.

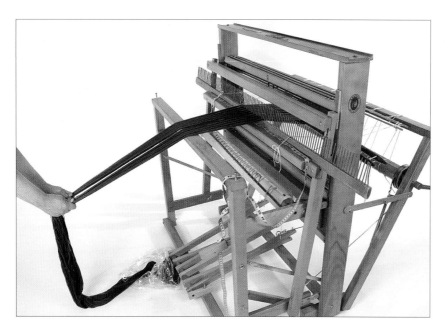

Your helper's hands become a clamp on the warp.

Next, put the brake on, so that the warp beam will turn toward you without being able to unwind. The warp yarn will go over the back beam and down onto the warp beam and wind up in one direction only.

Stand behind the loom. Wind the warp onto the beam slowly. You will drag your helper forward as you wind up the warp. Do not let the warp slip through the helper's hands. Have the helper maintain constant and even tension on the warp as you wind.

Make sure that the warp is winding straight and evenly. When your helper is at the loom and can't move forward any more, you will need to move the cross sticks forward. Put your hands on the cross sticks and with a finger in between the two sticks, slide the sticks forward toward the harnesses. They should slide smoothly in the cross slings. If you feel resistance, there is probably a loose thread that will need to be moved down into your helper's hand. When you have slid the cross sticks forward and your helper's hands are up to the breast beam or the front of the loom, ask the helper to drop the warp. Nothing will happen to the yarns that are already stored on the warp beam. The brake will keep the beam from unwinding.

Have the helper pick up a section of warp as far away from the front of the loom as is practical and repeat the preparation process as before. Do this over and over again until you have wound most of the warp onto the beam. Wind the warp onto the back beam when the warp is smooth and even, as in the first steps. Again, when your helper reaches the front of the loom, move the cross sticks forward. If you can move them forward easily, you are ready to beam the next length of warp.

If the cross sticks do not move forward easily, you must clear any loose threads that are caught. Do this by separating the threads at the cross from side to side, not up and down. Keep milking any loose threads toward the helper's hands and having them smooth the warp threads until you can easily move the cross sticks forward.

Wind on the new amount and repeat the process until you have stored all but that last few feet of the warp. As the warp is stored on the warp beam, place strips of wood, known as lath slats, in the warp as you wind it on the beam. This keeps the warp even and flat on the beam and allows the layers of warp to stay flat and under tension. You may also use corrugated cardboard; just make sure the sticks or the cardboard are wider than the warp you are winding. Wind the warp onto the warp beam until your helper can no longer hold the ends.

You will need to leave enough warp so that the cut ends of the warp reach just to the breast beam of the loom.

Once the warp is safely stored on the warp beam, take each section and tie a slip knot at the end of it.

The warp will look like this when you've tied all the ends.

Let each section of the warp fall behind the harnesses and dangle from the cross sticks. The raddle will then be free from the warp. To remove the raddle and move the cross sticks, first untie the cross slings from around the raddle. Be careful not to drop the cross sticks. Untie one sling and move it so that the raddle is free. Tie a bow holding one side of the cross sticks around the castle of the loom. Do the same to the other cross sling. The raddle can now be removed. If you used the beater cap to keep the inch sections in place, it can also be removed at this point.

Threading a Pattern

You are now ready to thread a pattern. The most logical and simple threading is called a "straight draw." This means that you will draw one thread through one heddle on each harness in order and repeat this order until you have threaded every thread in the warp.

If you had two harnesses, you would thread the first thread on harness 1 and the second thread on harness 2, and then you would thread the third thread back on harness 1 and the fourth thread on harness 2, and then continue in this pattern.

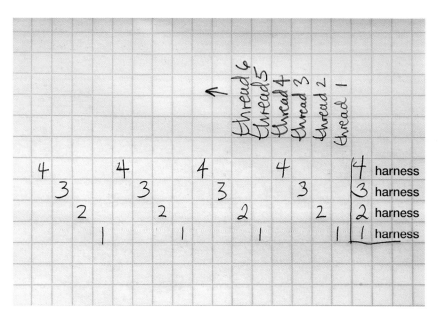

When you have four harnesses on the loom, you thread the first thread through the first harness, the second thread through the second harness, the third thread through the third harness, and the fourth thread through the fourth harness. You then thread the fifth thread through the first harness again. You will continue this pattern, or straight draw, until all the threads of the warp are threaded through one heddle on one harness, in order one through four, repeated over and over again.

back beam

warp
beam

Preliminary Steps for Threading the Loom

Slide the cross sticks as close to the harnesses as you can. You may need to rehang the cross slings so that the cross is at a good viewing level for you while you are sitting and threading.

Return to the front of the loom and release the hooks on all the harnesses.

Follow these steps and you will be ready to begin threading a pattern.

- If the breast beam can be taken off the loom, take it off.
- If the beater cap is still on, take it off.
- Find a chair that allows you to sit at the height of the harness as comfortably as you can. You can place books under the harnesses to raise them to a height that will make it easy for you to see the eyes of the heddles.
- Push the heddles you will need to the left side of the harnesses.
- With your right hand, slide one heddle from each harness to the right, in line with the right side of the warp on your warp beam.
- Take the first inch of warp, put it on the left side of these four heddles, and undo its slip knot, as shown in the top photo.

You will now select one thread from the rightmost side of the cross and thread it. It doesn't matter which thread in the group you choose. The cross keeps the order of the threads until they pass through the heddles. Once threaded, the heddles maintain the order of the threads.

Some weavers prefer using a threading hook to thread the heddles. Others just use their hands. Some weavers thread several ends at a time with a sleying hook. On the following pages are the steps for all three threading methods to help you decide which choice is best for you.

Threading with a Hook

Learning to use a threading hook from the start will be very useful in the long run. Allow the hook to separate the first two threads that are in the right-most position on the cross sticks.

Use the hook in the down position and pull one thread through the heddle on harness 1.

Push that heddle to the right and put your hook through the first heddle on harness 2. Select the next available thread in the cross. Pull that thread through the heddle and push the heddle to the right. Continue doing this until you have threaded the first four threads. Make sure each thread has a straight path from the back of the loom to the front of the loom. Move those threaded heddles to the right and select four more heddles in the same order, threading through harnesses 1, 2, 3, and 4 in order. Continue taking threads from the cross and threading them in order through the heddles until you have threaded all the threads in the warp.

Threading Multiple Ends with a Sleying Hook

Use this method after you've gained some confidence in your weaving. This method will help you thread patterns more efficiently. You will need a sleying hook.

Put the hook through the first heddle on harness 1, pick up the first thread with the hook, and slide the thread through the heddle. Leave the thread looped on the shaft of the hook.

Put the hook into the next heddle on harness 2. Pick up the next thread with the hook and put it through the heddle, leaving it looped on the shaft of the hook.

Go to harness 3 and thread it as in the previous step.

Go to harness 4 and thread it. All four threads are now on the hook ready to be pulled through.

Pull all the ends through at the same time. Each thread will be through its own heddle on its own harness. Move those threaded heddles to the right and select four more heddles in the same order. Continue in this order until you have threaded all the threads in the warp.

Threading without a Hook

In some cases, it can be fast and effective to thread by using your left hand to form a loop, poking it through the heddle, and passing the loop to your right hand. This method works especially well with textured yarns that can get caught on a hook.

Hold the group of threads in your left hand. Reach around with your right hand and select the first available thread, and then bend it into a loop and pass it into your left hand. The left hand, while still holding the other threads, pushes the loop through the heddle eye and the right hand pulls it the rest of the way through the heddle.

Pass the thread from the back of the heddle through the eye to the front into your right hand. Continue doing this until you have threaded the first four threads. Move those threaded heddles to the right and select four more heddles in the same order, threading through harnesses 1, 2, 3, and 4 in order. Continue this pattern until you have threaded all the threads in the warp.

As You Thread

After you slide the threaded heddles to the right, tie off groups of threaded warp ends in inches or small groups, using a slip knot. Pushing the groups to the right will give you a clear view of the heddles that you are threading. Move to your left as the threading progresses. If for some reason you lose your cross, don't panic. It's okay if a few threads cross each other. Take the threads in the order they appear, as close to straight as possible.

Moving Heddles from One Harness to Another

You can move heddles from harness to harness as needed if you run out of heddles on one harness. You will need either stiff wire or two heddles that will serve as transfer sticks.

1. Take a piece of stiff wire or a heddle.

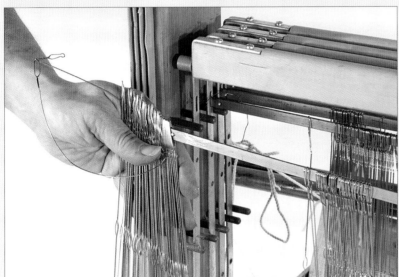

2. Slide it into the heddle tops that you want to move.

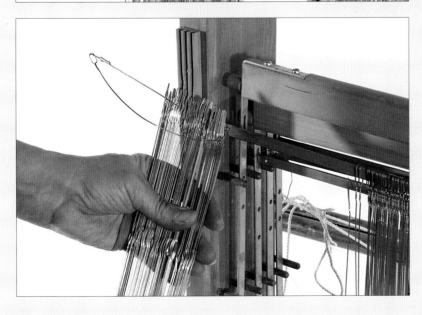

3. Make a circle with the wire so that those heddles are on both the wire and the harness bar.

4. Do the same at the bottom. Make sure you pick up all of the heddles.

5. Unfasten the harness bar, pull the harness bar out of its slot, and remove all the heddles that are on the wire. Replace the bar and fasten it.

6. Do the same at the bottom.

Be sure to check the other end
of the harness to make sure the
harness bar has not slipped out of
the fastener on the other end from
where you are removing heddles.
    You can also reverse this
process to add heddles to the
harness bars. Unfasten the top
bar, slide the heddles on, and then
redo the bar. Then do the bottom
in the same way. Try not to move
heddles individually.

Sleying the Reed

Once you have threaded all the ends of your warp through the heddles, you will sley the reed. Here are the tools you will need:

- A 10-, 12-, or 15-dent reed, the most common and most useful for handweaving
- A sleying hook, which is often different from a threading hook
- A tape measure

First pick the appropriate reed with the correct number of dents, or openings, to correspond with the density of the warp you will be weaving. Place the reed in the beater and secure the beater cap.

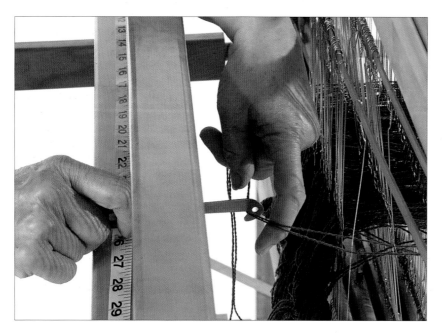

Take a tape measure and find the center of the loom and the center of the reed. Measure to the right half of the distance you will want for the width of your project.

Untie the first group of threaded ends at the right of your loom. Insert your hook in the dent or slot that is appropriate.

Take the first available thread or threads and draw them through the slot.

Here the first two threads have been drawn though the reed. The density of the warp dictates how many threads will come through each dent in a reed. If you are using a 12-dent reed and your density is 24 ends per inch (or EPI), then you will draw two threads through the dent. If the density is 12 EPI, then you will put one thread through each dent. If the density is 6 EPI, then you will put one thread through every other dent. If the density is higher, say 36 EPI, then you would put three threads through each dent. You can also sley combinations. So, for example, in a 12-dent reed with 28 EPI density, you can sley two threads through the first dent you have chosen, then two threads through the next dent, and then three threads through the next dent. Then repeat 2, 2, and 3 again, and keep repeating that pattern: 2, 2, 3, 2, 2, 3.

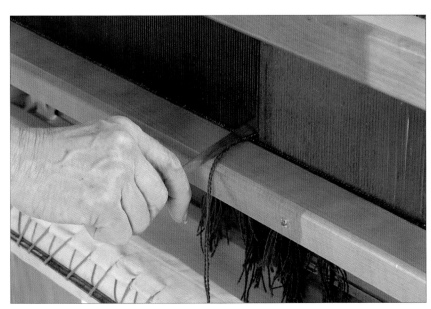

Continuing with the 12-dent reed for this example, and working your way from right to left, take the next two threads in your warp in your sleying hook and draw them through the next dent in the reed.

I reach my left arm over the top of the beater cap in order to stabilize the beater and to present the next threads to the sleying hook.

Again tie small groups with slip knots. This will keep the beater from falling forward and pulling out what you have already sleyed.

Continue until all the warp ends are through the reed.

Make a clear path in line with the harness hooks so that no heddles are caught on one side at the top and the other side of the hooks at the bottom. Then rehook the harness hooks. This is easier to do if you move the heddles far away from the hooks.

Tying on to the Cloth Apron

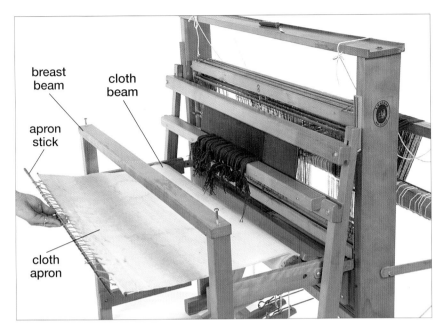

Now we are ready to tie the warp onto the cloth apron so that we can begin weaving. If you have removed your breast beam, put it back on now. It is best to remove the cross sticks at this point. They have served their purpose and the heddles and the reed now hold the position of the threads. Open one end of the cross sticks and slide them out from the warp.

Bring the apron and apron stick up over the breast beam.

Grab the warp and give it a light shake toward you to line up the heddles.

Take a small group of threads of about an inch from the middle of your warp. Untie the slip knot. Split the group into two parts. Bring each part over the apron stick between any string or division of cloth. Bring each part under and back up so that the tails are on the outside of each part.

Tie these together into a half knot or half of a surgeon's knot.

Do the same for a small group at each edge of the warp. Go back to the center and tie small groups starting from the middle and working to the edges.

When you have all of the warp tied to the apron, go back to the middle and tighten up all the knots.

Finish them into a square knot.

You want even tension on all of the warp threads. Feel with your hand to make sure this is the case. Retie any knots that are loose or slack. Go to the back of the loom and make sure everything looks even and smooth.

Tying up the Treadles

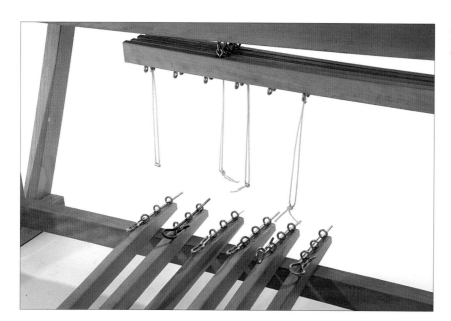

Every loom has a different system for doing this, but it's an easy process.

Now that the warp is beamed, threaded, sleyed, and tied onto the apron, you are ready to tie up the treadles in a pattern so that the harnesses can be moved up and down.

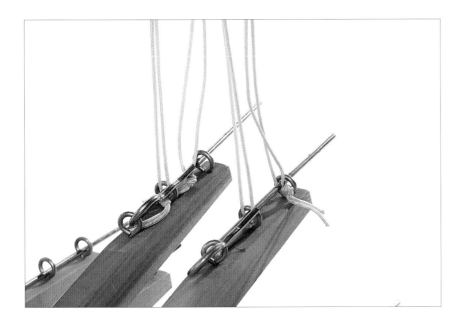

The first tie-up will give us plain weave. You start by tying the two middle treadles. One treadle will be tied to harness 1 and harness 3. The other treadle will be tied to harness 2 and harness 4. For the first project we will use a common and useful tie-up.

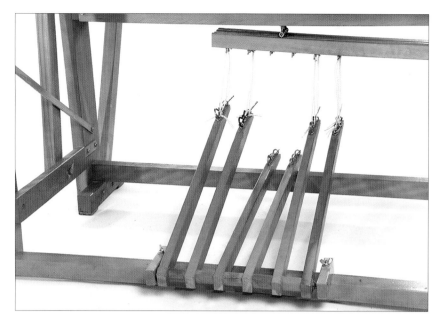

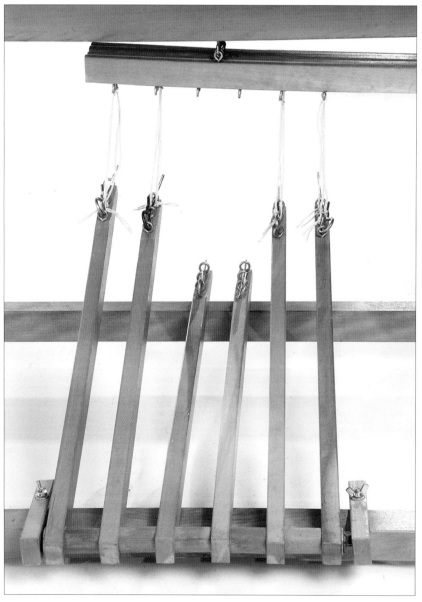

Work from the front of the loom and do the following:

1. First treadle on the left: Tie to harness 1 and harness 2.
2. First treadle on the right: Tie to harness 2 and harness 3.
3. Next treadle in on the left: Tie to harness 3 and harness 4.
4. Next treadle in on the right: Tie to harness 1 and harness 4.
5. The two middle treadles: Tie the one on the left to harness 1 and harness 3.
6. Tie the last treadle to harness 2 and harness 4.

In this way we have what are referred to as the pattern harness tie-ups on the four outside treadles, leaving the two center treadles to weave plain weave (over one thread, under the next thread). We have also set up the sequence so that when we are weaving with a single shuttle in twill weave, we can throw with our left hand and step on one of the left treadles, and when we throw from the right we will use one of the right treadles.

This system of stepping left and right alternately is one that was used by weavers in the seventeenth and eighteenth centuries and is very useful and balanced.

The Filling

Now it is time to talk about the yarn that will go across the warp. This is sometimes called the "weft," but for our purposes we will use the word "filling." You will *fill* the quill, or bobbin, with yarn and you will *fill* up the spaces in the warp. You will need the following tools:

- A bobbin winder
- 5 to 10 plastic or wooden bobbins
- 2 or 3 boat shuttles

Winding a Bobbin

With a cone of yarn on the floor, mount your bobbin winder at a height that is easy to use.

Put the bobbin on the spindle and make sure that it is tight.

Start winding in the center of the bobbin with as much tension on your yarn as you can bear. Some people use a piece of leather to prevent them from burning their fingers.

Go smoothly from one side to the other, winding the bobbin as tightly as possible and as smoothly as possible.

End in the middle of the bobbin. Think of a sewing machine bobbin and try to keep the yarn as flat and even as possible. The smoother and more even the bobbin, the better it will unwind in the weaving process.

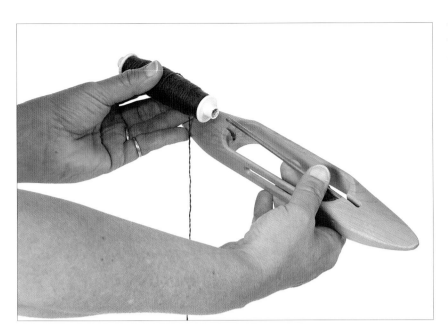

Take a boat shuttle and place the bobbin in the cavity, with some yarn unwound underneath.

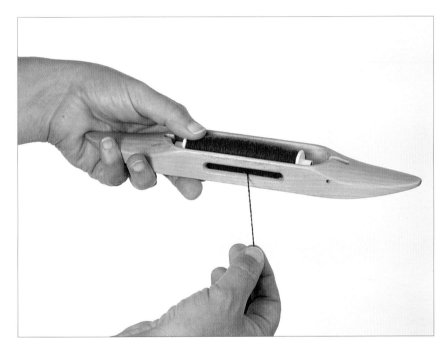

The yarn must pass through the fare lead, the hole in the side of the shuttle.

Sitting down to Weave

Now you are ready to begin weaving. You will need the following tools:

- Pins
- A pick glass
- Scissors
- Duct tape
- A weaving bench

Find a bench or chair that is at a height that allows you to be above the breast beam so that you can have your arms free for weaving.

With the beater in its backmost position, step on the brake and at the same time lift up on the handle that controls the cloth beam. Release the warp from the warp beam at the same time that you crank forward on the cloth beam so that your apron stick is at the breast beam. This will give you room to begin weaving. Release your brake on the warp beam a little bit before you stop cranking forward to get the tension that you will need for weaving. It is better to weave with a tight warp than a loose warp, but too tight will not allow the harnesses to rise properly and may lead to broken warp threads. Too loose a warp will result in uneven tensions and sagging warp threads that will not raise or lower when they should. Practice will teach what the proper tension is.

Holding the shuttle in your left hand with the opening facing you, step on the third treadle in from the left side. Press it as far down as it will go. When you step on a treadle, the harnesses should move so that there will be a space between the threads that are up and the threads that are down. This space is called "the shed." The shed is where you will send the shuttle back and forth across the warp.

For the first throw, leave a tail of the yarn that is on the bobbin in the shuttle hanging out, and place the shuttle into the shed on the left side of the loom. You will only leave a tail to begin. Always have the beater in the backmost position when the shuttle goes through the shed. Continue to hold the treadle down.

Send the shuttle across the warp in the shed against the reed. Have your right hand in a position with the palm up and the thumb out to receive the shuttle. Your index finger will be on the tip of the shuttle ready to send the shuttle back for the next throw. Take your left hand and place it on the beater in the middle. Bring the beater forward toward you until the reed pushes the first thread or pick toward the knots of the warp on the apron stick. When you first start it will not look like a woven piece until you have woven a few inches. Return the beater to the back position. Step with your right foot on the treadle that is three in from the right side.

With the beater in the back position and the shed open, send the shuttle back across the warp. Have your left hand with the palm up and the thumb out and the index finger ready to catch the shuttle.

As you send the shuttle across, the bobbin will unwind. Do not pull the bobbin. Do not stop the bobbin from unwinding. Throw the shuttle against the reed, and once the shuttle is past the warp, beat the thread in place gently by just pressing the beater and reed against the last throw of the shuttle.

Do not worry about the edges of the cloth or the evenness of the beat until you have woven a few inches and the spaces between the knots have come together.

Projects

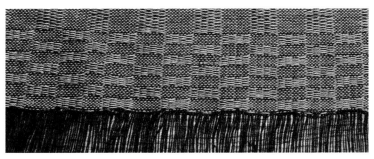

When asked by beginning weavers for advice, I give them these pointers:

- Do samples of your projects first.
- Keep an accurate notebook with your drafts, yarns, and setts.
- Keep a sample of everything you weave and put it into your notebook with your notes.

I advise weavers to sample as many different types of pattern weavings as they can before attempting weaving projects. This book offers you four different projects that build on some aspect of pattern weaving and employ techniques that are the essential ingredients in weaving. The four projects include almost all the basic weave structures, which handweavers can then expand on.

A Word about Woven Patterns

There are basically two systems that allow weavers to weave patterns into cloth regardless of color and texture: twill weaves and block weaves.

Twill weaves produce small overall designs in which diagonal lines create the patterns. Jean twill, which is a 2/1 twill, is the simplest.

The more harnesses one has, the more complex the twill work can be, so by adding harnesses, weavers can make complicated ratios of overs and unders.

A complex twill weave might be diagrammed like this:

$$2\ 3\ 1$$
$$2\ 4\ 3$$

This means that the pattern consists of throwing the shuttle over 2 warp ends, then under 2 warp ends, over 3, under 4, over 1, under 4. If we add up the overs and unders, we get 16 harnesses necessary to create this twill.

You can reverse twills in the threading or the treadling to make zigzags. You can also reverse twills in both the threading and the treadling and make diamonds. This can be done on any scale given a number of harnesses. On four harnesses, however, twill weaving is somewhat limited.

The other patterning device is block weaving, and there are many weave structures that give us design blocks that we can work with.

Ms and Os, spot weave, tied spot weave (also called Bronson lace), and float work (sometimes referred to as overshot) are all examples of block weaves that allow us to create pattern designs using from 2 to 4 blocks.

The Count System

Yarn comes in different sizes, and each type of yarn—wool, cotton, linen, worsted wool, silk, rayon—has a different numbering system. For your purposes, you want to know how many yards to 1 pound there will be in the yarn we are using for a project.

The count number is usually the higher number, so in the 2/8 worsted wool yarn called for in Project 1, the count number is 8. The ply number, the 2 here, is usually small, because we are usually using either a single-ply yarn, listed as a 1, or a two-ply yarn, marked as a 2. So a yarn labeled 2/8 means that there are 2 plies of number 8 worsted in that yarn.

Number 8 worsted is 8 times as *fine* as number 1 worsted. In other words, the higher the second number, the finer the yarn. 2/24 yarn is finer than 2/8 yarn, for example.

The count number for worsted is 560 yards to the pound, so 8 times 560 equals 4,480 yards to the pound, but you have to divide by 2 because you have a two-ply yarn. So really you have 2,240 yards in 1 pound of 2/8 worsted.

There is a table on page 107 that gives you the standard count numbers and also the yards per pound for common yarn counts, just to make it easier for you. Refer to this table when you are calculating how much yarn you will need for a project.

Tip: Never skimp on the cost of good yarn. Bad yarn makes bad cloth and is more trouble than it's worth. Buy yarn directly from good suppliers. You will be more successful and not get frustrated by yarns that break.

Straight Draw, Reversing Draw, and Regularly Reversing Draw on 12 Shafts

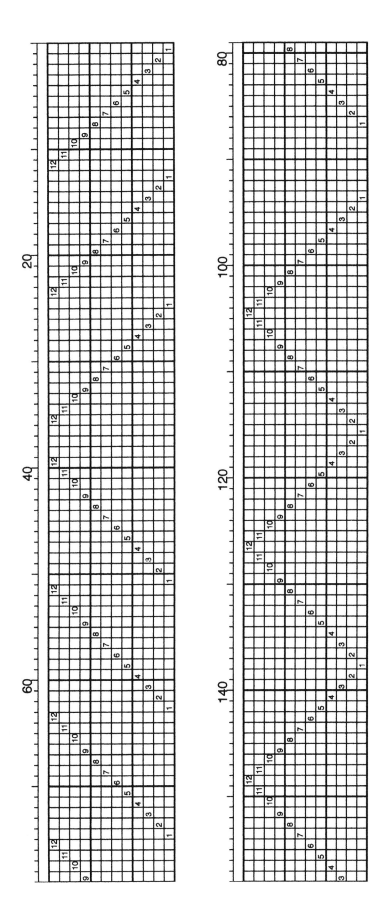

PROJECT 1

Two-Color Checked Scarf in Worsted Wool

Your first project is a two-color, plain-weave checked scarf in worsted wool. What is worsted wool? It is *not* what knitters use to make sweaters or mittens. For weavers, worsted wool means a smooth yarn in which the fibers are from a long-staple fleece and are spun parallel to each other to create a smooth yarn. Men's suits and Scottish kilts are examples of garments made from worsted wool. Worsted wool is smoother and silkier than woolen yarns, which are fuzzy and make good blankets and sweaters.

Materials

- 2 pounds of 2/8 worsted wool in a green or blue
- 1 pound of 2/8 worsted wool in a different color. (I will use maroon.) You will need less of this wool, but having a pound will give you plenty to work with. I use Jagger Spun worsted wool.

Making Your Yarn Calculations

Because this is your first project, I am giving you the *sett*, which means the number of warp threads you will need in 1 inch. I am also telling you how many inches of width you will need to make the scarf. Neither of these numbers is written in stone.

You may try this same project using a thicker yarn or a thinner yarn and adjust the number of warp ends per inch (EPI) to suit your taste. This is where sampling first is very helpful. You may also want a wider or narrower scarf. For the purposes of learning, here are the figures used in the calculations for this project:

- You are going to make two scarves and a sample for your notebook.
- Each scarf will finish 78 inches long and have 6 inches of fringe on each end, so we will need 12 inches of fringe for each scarf.
- Each scarf will be 12 inches wide on the loom.
- The sett is 24 EPI, meaning each inch will contain 24 warp ends.

Calculation is easier than it sounds when we are beginning. You need the length of the two scarves and their fringes.

- 78 inches + 12 inches = 90 inches x 2 scarves = 180 inches total, or 5 yards.

This is the length of warp you will need for the scarves; however, we will need more than just this amount. There are three important additions to our total length:

- Loom waste. This is the amount of the warp that you don't actually get to weave. The very beginning of the warp needs to be tied onto the apron of the cloth beam, and the very end of the warp cannot get woven, because there is not enough length to make a shed for the shuttle. Loom waste varies somewhat depending on your loom. For now, you will consider 1 yard a sufficient amount to account for loom waste, and that will also give you enough extra so that you can make samples to put in your notebook.
- Take-up. This is the loss in length of warp yarn as it travels over and under the filling yarn.
- Shrinkage. You must also include shrink rate, which is the loss of length when you take a piece off the loom. The warp is under tension and it contracts when you release the tension and take it off the loom, so you must add some length to compensate for that.

So, this is how you calculate the length of warp you need for this project:

- Scarves: 90 inches x 2 scarves = 180 inches, or 5 yards
- + 1 yard for loom waste = 6 yards
- + 10 percent of the current 6 yards total (.1 x 6) for take-up = 6.6 yards
- + 10 percent of the current 6.6 yards total (.1 x 6.6) for shrinkage = 7.26 yards

So if you round the warp to 8 yards long, you will have plenty for two scarves, loom waste, take-up, shrinkage, and a sample.

To calculate how many ends you need, take the number of ends in each inch of the warp and multiply it by the width of your project. The sett is 24 EPI and the width of the scarf is 12 inches, so you will multiply these two figures:

- 24 EPI x 12 inches = 288 ends, each one 8 yards long

Now, to calculate how much yarn you need, multiply the total length of the warp by the total number of ends in the warp:

- 8 yards x 288 ends = 2,304 yards

Although that seems like a big number (and it is!), don't be intimidated. In weaving you'll use many, many yards of yarn. The 2,304 yards you need is a little more than 1 pound of 2/8 worsted wool. How do you find how many yards there are in 1 pound of a yarn? You can either look at the yarn count table or do the math.

In a 2/8 worsted wool, you have 8 x 560 (the count number) divided by 2 (the ply number) so you know that there are a total of 2,240 yards in 1 pound of 2/8 worsted wool yarn.

If you were weaving with only one color, you would need more than a pound of this yarn for the warp. But you will be using two colors for the warp and two colors for the filling. The warping pattern here will be 20 threads of green and then 4 threads of maroon. Feel free to use any color combination that suits your taste. You will start by winding 20 ends of green and 4 ends of maroon, then 20 ends of green and 4 ends of maroon, and you will do that 11 times. To finish the scarf and make it look balanced, you will add another 20 ends of green. This will be just shy of 12 inches wide. You will have 11 stripes of maroon, each with 4 threads, so some of the warp will be maroon and the rest will be green.

Setting Up

- Refer to the Basic Skills chapter when setting up the yarn for winding the warp. Set up two cones of green and one cone of maroon, so that it is easy to wind the yarns onto your warping reel.

- Change from the green warp yarn to the maroon warp yarn as you are winding.
- Wrap the green yarn around the last peg at least twice. This will hold it from slipping and keep its tension. Cut it between the cone and the wrap. Unwind it and tie the maroon on with an overhand knot, tying the two green ends to the one maroon end.
- You must unwind it so that the length of the warp is the same and continuous. Have the knot fall at the peg, not into your cross. Wind the maroon so that you have 4 threads of maroon. Wind it around the top peg, cut it, and tie the 2 ends of green onto the one end of maroon. Do this 11 times, and then finish by winding 20 ends of green.
- End your warp by making a loop large enough to put your finger in.
- Tie a cross.
- Tie a working loop through the head end of the warp, catching the first and last loop, and get your loom ready to beam.
- Go through the steps in the Basic Skills chapter for beaming on, threading (see drafts on page 75), sleying the reed, tying onto the cloth apron, setting up the treadles, and winding the bobbins.

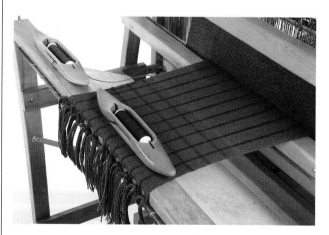

Remember that you are using two colors, so that means you will need two shuttles and at least two bobbins.

Weaving the First Scarf in Plain Weave

Now you are ready to weave your first scarf. The scarf will be woven in a 1/1 plain weave. Use the two treadles in the center of your loom.

- Tie the left treadle to harnesses 1 and 3 and the right treadle to harnesses 2 and 4. Remember to step left when you are throwing the shuttle from the left side and step right to open the shed when you are throwing from the right side.

Plain Weave Checked Scarf

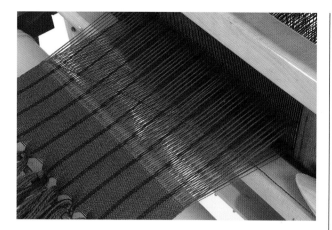

- Note the fringe for this end of the scarf will be the warp ends that you have tied onto your apron.

- Start weaving with your green yarn. It will take a little while before it looks like cloth. If the shuttle is in your left hand, step left and throw it. When the shuttle is in your right hand, step right, make your shed, and throw the shuttle.

- After about 2 inches, the gaps from tying should close, and you should be making cloth. At this point, you will need a tape measure and a linen tester. Stop and count the number of throws of the shuttle, called "picks," in 1 inch of your cloth. You should have about 18 to 22 threads. This number will vary and your filling thread count, or pick count, will become more and more consistent as you get better at the rhythm of weaving. In plain weave, you will want the same number of picks in 1 inch horizontally as you have threads vertically in the warp. But remember that you are weaving with threads under tension, so when the cloth relaxes when you take it off the loom, it will gain about 2 picks per inch.

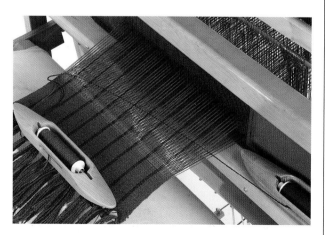

- After you have thrown the green for 2 inches, put down the green shuttle. Do *not* cut or break off the green filling yarn.

- Now pick up the maroon shuttle, leaving a tail hanging out of the shed, and throw the shuttle in the new shed. Always start and stop both shuttles on the same side of the loom. I usually start on the left and finish on the left, as it is typical to do an even number of picks or throws of the shuttle.

- As you begin the second throw of the maroon shuttle, tuck the end of the yarn from the start of the maroon into the shed on the left-hand side. Bring it in a few warp threads and leave it in the shed to be pushed in place when you send the maroon shuttle back.

- After making 4 picks of maroon, place that shuttle down, and pick up the green shuttle again. Do *not* cut the maroon yarn; leave it attached. You only have an end when the bobbin runs out.

- Check your pick count often by using the linen tester to count the number of picks in 1 inch of your cloth. I pin a tape measure to the cloth as I weave so that I can keep an accurate count of woven inches; however, you can measure and place a pin in your cloth and mark the number of inches on a piece of paper if you prefer. Do whatever works best for you.

- Advance the warp often and keep your weaving space within a small area. Do not weave as close as you can to the reed and then advance the warp close to the breast beam, because this makes for irregular selvages (finished edges) and an irregular beat. A 3- or 4-inch weaving space is quite enough.

- When you are done weaving the 78 inches you need for your first scarf, set your two shuttles aside.

- Advance your warp 6 inches. This will be the fringe on the first scarf. Leave it unwoven. Throw two throws of either shuttle as a cutting line. Then advance the warp again another 6 inches. This will be the fringe on your next scarf. Leave this 6 inches unwoven as well.

Weaving the Second Scarf in Twill Weave

thread 6
thread 5
thread 4
thread 3
thread 2
thread 1

```
 4        4        4        4       4
   3        3        3        3     3
     2        2        2        2   2
_____
     3   1   3   1   3   1   3   1  1    3
 4     2   4   2   4   2   4   2      2  4
   3   1   3   1   3   1   3   1      1  3
 4     2   4   2   4   2   4   2      2  4
   x   x   x   x   x   x   x   x      1  3
 x     x   x   x   x   x   x   x      2  4

     2 1     2 1     2 1     2 1  1  2
   3 2     3 2     3 2     3 2       2 3
 4 3     4 3     4 3     4 3         3 4
 4       1 4     1 4     1 4      1  1    4
     2 1     2 1     2 1     2 1  1  2
   3 2     3 2     3 2     3 2       2 3
 4 3     4 3     4 3     4 3         3 4
 4       1 4     1 4     1 4      1  1    4
     x x     x x     x x     x x  1  2
   x x     x x     x x     x x      2 3
 x x     x x     x x     x x        3 4
 x       x x     x x     x x      x  1    4
```

Now that you have woven one scarf in plain weave, you can weave another scarf in a twill weave. The common twill used on four-harness looms is a balanced twill of 2/2, which means that each filling thread goes over 2 warp ends and then under 2 warp ends. Remember that while the ratio does not change, twills progress by one warp end, either to the left or to the right.

On threading, which is a straight draw, the progression will be straight. You will move harnesses 1 and 2 together, then harnesses 2 and 3 together (thus progressing one warp end), then harnesses 3 and 4 together, and finally harnesses 4 and 1 together. Tie your treadles so that you can step with your left foot when you throw the shuttle with your left hand, and step with your right foot when you throw the shuttle with your right hand. There are four steps or picks to repeat this twill.

- Tie the outside left treadle to harnesses 1 and 2.
- Tie the outside right treadle to harnesses 2 and 3.
- Tie the inside left treadle to harnesses 3 and 4.
- Tie the inside right treadle to harnesses 1 and 4.

Tip: Twills are directional, which means that if one or two of your selvage threads are not being picked up at all, even after throwing the four picks of a repeat, you may change the direction that you start your twill. To correct this problem, you can change the direction that the shuttle is going, or you can rethread the last threads on that side of the loom, so that the threading is 1, 3, 4, 2.

Taking the Scarves Off the Loom

On handlooms, you cannot cut off one scarf without retying the warp to the cloth beam apron again. If you want to cut off one scarf at a time in the future, you must plan enough loom waste to retie the warp onto the apron and begin weaving again.

If you weave the scarves as a continuous length you will weave to the end of your warp. The apron stick that attaches to the warp beam can be advanced until you can no longer make a good shed.

Cut the warp threads at the back of the loom and pull them through your harness. Unhook the cloth beam ratchet so that you can unwind the scarves from the cloth beam.

Take the entire length of the web and lay it on a table and separate the scarves at the cutting lines that you put in during weaving. Now you are ready to finish your scarves by tying fringe.

2/2 Twill Weave Checked Scarf

Tying Fringe for a Scarf

There are two different ways to tie fringe that are equally pleasing: a simple knotted fringe and a plied fringe.
To start, put a weight on the scarf so that you can pull against the end without moving it.

Simple Knotted Fringe

1. Start at the right end of the scarf and pick up 4 or 5 warp ends. Twist them tightly.
2. At the top end of the fringe toward the scarf, make a small overhand knot and sink it right to the edge of the scarf.
3. Repeat this across the entire edge.
4. Comb the fringe and trim it to an even length.

Plied Fringe

This style was often used on traditional Scottish shawls.

1. Start on the right end of the scarf and pick up two groups of warp ends, each having 4 or 5 yarns.
2. Twist each group independently, very tightly, so that they kink.
3. Maintain tension equally on the two twists.

4. Holding both groups at the bottom, twist them together in the opposite direction from the way you twisted them individually.

5. Tie a knot at the bottom end in the place where you want the fringe to end. You may leave the knots or cut them off.
6. You may need to steam or press the fringe to maintain it without the knot at the end.

Finishing the Scarves

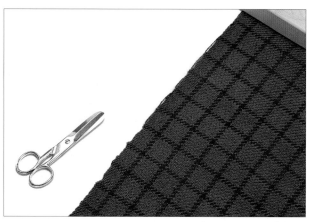

As you were weaving, you carried the filling yarns up one side of your scarf. It's now time to clip these carry-ups as close to the selvage as you can. Do not cut into the warp of the scarf.

Here is the finished plain-weave scarf. Since we wove the scarves using worsted wool, we don't want to wash them. Instead, steam and press them. That will relax the yarns and allow the softness and luster of the worsted to show.

PROJECT 2

Ms and Os Cotton Placemat and Runner Set

Ms and Os is a version of a rib weave and a plain weave that is very versatile. It has a historic precedent but can be used in many ways with different types of yarns in modern weaving. The letters resemble what the woven pattern looks like.

New in This Project

- Reading a pattern draft: This project will help you to understand pattern threading and two-block designs
- Balancing a pattern so that the design is aesthetically pleasing
- Making several pieces of the same size so that you have a set of placemats and a runner

Materials

- 1 pound of 10/2 colored cotton, mercerized or unmercerized
- 1 pound of 10/2 cotton in a lighter tone than the first color

The Threading Draft

No matter what pattern threading draft you come upon, it is always a good idea to try to get a sense of the rhythm of the threading. This will tell you a lot about what the pattern will create.

With this Ms and Os project you have your first pattern draft that has several units or parts to make the pattern, so you must understand the units of Ms and Os. Although Ms and Os is based on plain weave, it is one of the few patterns in which you cannot easily weave a one–over-one plain weave all the way across the warp. That is because the units are based on opposites.

Ms and Os for Placemats

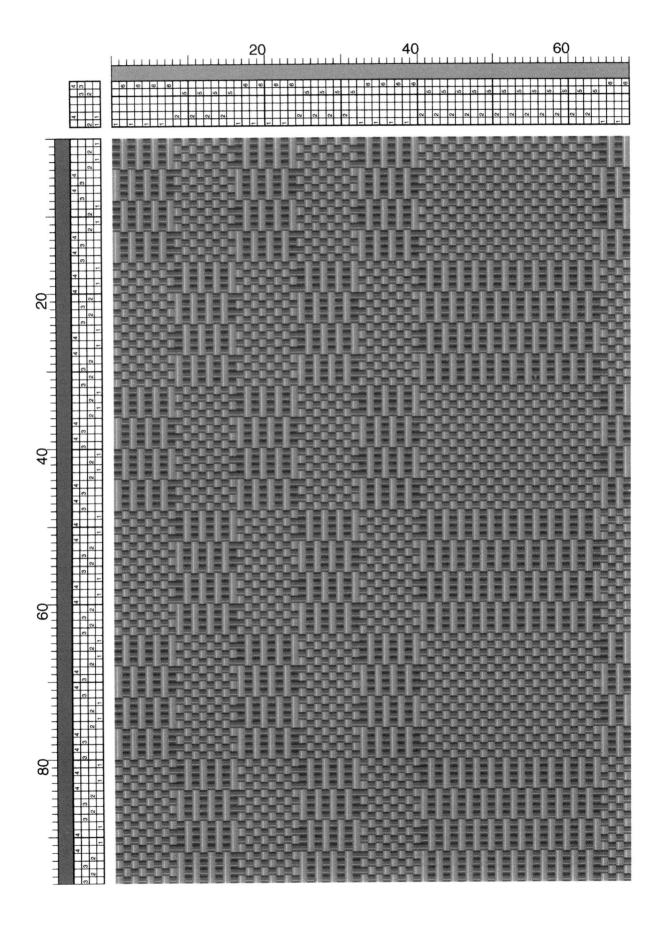

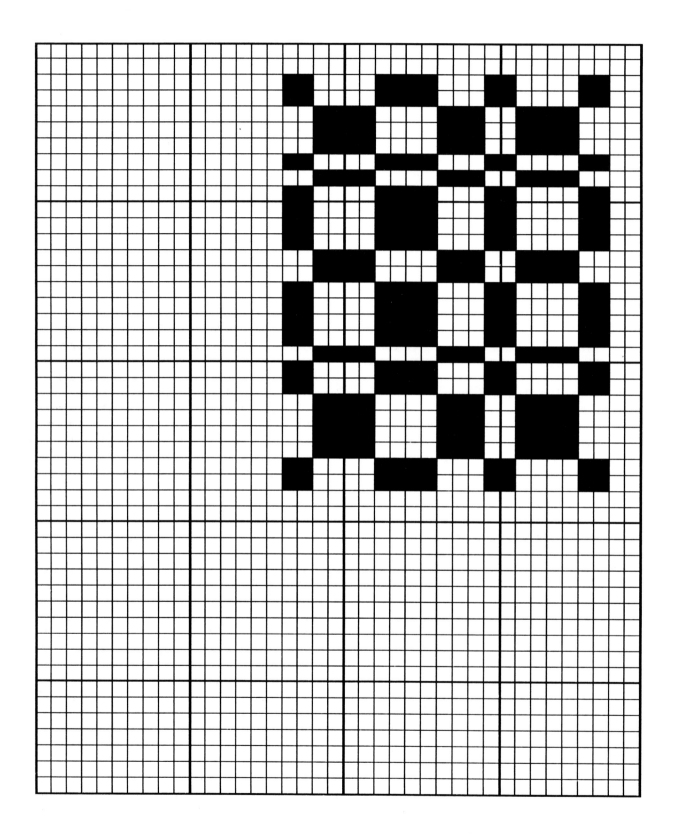

Two-Block Design

Historic Ms and Os

This bleached linen towel with initials was woven in simple Ms and Os around 1800. Ms and Os weaving appears in weavers' draft books as early as the seventeenth century and was called various names, including "MNO," "MM," and "OOs" or other combinations of these letters.

Ms and Os in its original form consists of weaving a 4/4 (four over and then four under) rib weave next to a 1/1 (one over one) plain weave and then switching these two blocks.

This is a two-block pattern, which means you can design using the two blocks as building blocks and make any combination of the blocks to create an almost unlimited number of designs—once you understand the basic units.

The two-block design can be illustrated on a sheet of graph paper. In woven block work, all the blocks that run up and down in a single line must have the same width, because they represent how that section of the warp was threaded. All of the blocks running in a horizontal line must have the same height because they represent how many times the shuttle is thrown across the warp for that block.

Warping

Wind a warp that has 24 ends in each inch. Make your warp 16 inches wide and 8 yards long. A good way to plan a balanced design is to total up the number of threads that you have in your warp.

• 24 EPI x 16 inches wide = 384 ends of warp

Plan a selvage of at least 4 ends for each side of the warp. In our case we will thread the first 4 and the last 4 ends in a straight draw of 1,2,3,4.

• 384 - 8 ends = 376 pattern ends

Now look at the threading draft and understand the units of pattern. This becomes increasingly more important as you progress through complex patterning. You have two units, each has 8 ends in the unit. You can call one block A and the other block B.

Block A will be threaded 1,2,1,2,4,3,4,3. What is important about this threading is the *jump* from the thread on harness 2 to the next thread entering on harness 4. So every time you want an A block you will thread all 8 ends exactly as I have laid them out.

Block B will be threaded 1,4,1,4,2,3,2,3. Notice again a *jump* from harness 4 to harness 2. That is why we cannot make plain weave across the warp from side to side without double ends at some points.

Now, the fun thing about this 2-block weave is that we can put as many A blocks or as many B blocks together in a row in the threading and in the treadling as we want in order to create designs.

So when you want to create a placemat with a border, you can put several A blocks in a row in the threading and then alternate block B and block A to create a center and balance the design on the other side with the border again.

Weavers write in many different styles. I prefer the modern style in which the harness number appears in the space that indicates where the thread will be placed. We know that we will thread the next available thread to the left, so numbering the threads seems silly. But there are shorthand and many other notations that work well for modern weavers. We also make notes about how many times to repeat a particular part of the draft to shorten the number of times we must write the same information.

There are several good computer programs for writing pattern drafts. I use Fiberworks PCW silver. (See Fiberworks Weaving Design Software, http://www.fiberworks-pcw.com.)

Threading

Here is your threading:

- Thread a 4-end selvage of straight draw 1,2,3,4
- Then thread 8 block As or 64 threads of A
- Then thread 2 blocks of B or 16 threads of B
- Because you are balancing this pattern, reserve the same number of threads on the other side of the warp for the selvage and the borders, so 4, 64, and 16.
- That leaves 27 units of 8 threads for the center, so begin threading A, then B, over and over, and end with A.
- Then thread 2 blocks of B, then 8 blocks of A, and then your selvage.

Tying up the Treadles

When you weave with a single shuttle, it is very convenient to place the treadle combinations on the loom in a way that allows you to "walk," meaning that when the shuttle is in your left hand, you step on a treadle on the left, and when the shuttle is in your right hand, you step on a treadle that is on the right side of the loom. Your feet alternate, so you are walking left, right, left, right, and so on. For Ms and Os there are two treadle combinations for each block.

For block A:

- Treadle 1 is tied to harness 1 and harness 2
- Treadle 4 is tied to harness 3 and harness 4

For block B:

- Treadle 2 is tied to harness 1 and harness 4
- Treadle 3 is tied to harness 2 and harness 3

You will treadle the combinations as many times as you threaded the combinations, so if you threaded block A with 8 threads, you will treadle block A eight times, if the size of your yarn for the filling is about the same size as your warp yarn.

If you threaded block B with 8 threads, you would do the same with the block B treadles, throwing the shuttle 8 times and alternating between treadle 2 and treadle 3.

As you weave the border where you have repeated block A several times, you will weave the block A combination as many times as you threaded the A block in the border.

Tip: Do not overbeat this weave structure. Send your shuttle across and gently "kiss" the filling into place. Your beat should be slightly less than the sett of the warp, so no more than 22 throws of the shuttle in 1 inch.

You make a web of unfinished cloth on the loom. The density will change when you take the cloth off and when

Detail of the Ms and Os placemat pattern in two colors.

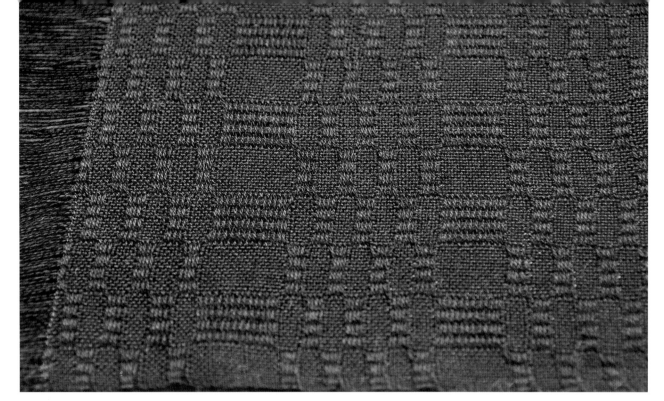

The runner has areas where one block is elongated to make a border.

you wash it. Usually it will gain at least two picks off the loom and shrink about another 15 percent, so do not overbeat when you are weaving.

When you begin a project that has multiples, a good way to keep track is to take a tape measure and pin it along the side of the cloth as you weave. Try to keep your tension the same each time you move your warp, and pin the tape measure in at least two places.

For the placemats, you will want a finished length of 19 inches, so you must weave about 22 inches in length. You also want a short fringe on each end. Leave 1 inch before you start the placemat and then leave another inch for fringe at the end of the 22 inches. Make sure you leave another inch to start the next placemat.

There are easy ways to keep the fringe length uniform. One way is to cut strips of thin cardboard that are all the same width and insert them as you would your shuttle into the shed, then change the shed and place the next cardboard strip into a new shed, and so on. Another way is simply to leave an area unwoven, then weave two picks, and leave another area unwoven, and then begin weaving your next placemat.

In the finishing, sew along the edge of the woven area to ensure that the fringe does not unravel.

I recommend that you weave a sample of the Ms and Os so that you know your beat and tension before you start weaving your first placemat. Try to keep your beat, the tension on your warp, and the amount you let off and take up every time as much the same as you can from placemat to placemat.

Weaving the Placemat

1. Start weaving using the same treadles that correspond to the first part of the threaded pattern for the border, which is block A repeated, so that there are about 64 throws of the shuttle. This should give you a border that is a square block having the same length as it has width. Look at the right and left sides of your weaving to see the border.
2. Next look to the inside upper corner of your border block and weave block B twice. That should be 16 picks, and it should create another smaller mini-border.
   Measure from the beginning to the end of the second block B. Write this number down. This is the length you will need to weave at the other end of the place-mat to make the mini-border and the corner.
3. Look to the inside upper corner of the B blocks, and you will now begin alternating one repeat of block A and then one repeat of block B until you have woven the center of the placemat.
4. End the center section with block A. You will need to weave the center the length of the placemat minus the beginning and end borders.

The total length of the placemat should be about 22 inches, not including the fringe.

Weaving the Runner

The runner is the same as the placemats, except that the center will be longer. Usually a runner is at least 44 inches long.

Weave your borders the same as you have for the placemats, but keep weaving in the center until it is about twice as long as the center of your placemats.

PROJECT 3

Herringbone-Checked Seamed Blanket

For this next project, you will be weaving the full width of the loom to create a two-color, herringbone-checked blanket. I am giving sett and calculations for a lightweight blanket and a heavyweight blanket. The width of your loom will determine whether you will weave two panels or three panels to fit a double bed. You will need two shuttles, one for each color.

New in This Project

- Weaving a full loom width
- Weaving panels that match in the center
- Using a template
- Weaving herringbone patterns
- Weaving diamond patterns

Lightweight Blanket

Materials

- 6 pounds Harrisville Designs Shetland Yarn (1,800 YPP) in one color (natural was used here)
- 4 pounds of Harrisville Designs Shetland Yarn in a different color (midnight blue here)

Sett and Calculations

The sett will be 16 EPI and your loom width will determine how wide a panel you can make.

- If your weaving width is 36 inches, plan your warp for 32 inches wide.
- If your weaving width is 45 inches, plan your warp width for 42 inches wide.

Weaving to the absolute maximum of your loom width is counterproductive. Weaving either extremely wide or extremely narrow is more difficult, so plan to weave slightly more narrow than the loom width. For a seamed blanket, 88 inches of finished length for each panel will fit a bed nicely. If you are working at a 32-inch width, you will need to weave three panels. If you are working on a 42-inch width, you can weave two panels.

Here are the calculations for a two-panel blanket:

- 2 panels x 88 inches long + 36 inches (for loom waste) + 20 percent (for shrinkage) = 7 yards

If you want to make a throw, add 3 yards, for a total length of 10 yards. To figure out how much yarn you will need, multiply your density by the width in inches and then multiply that by the length of your warp.

Historic Checks

Made in Schoharie County, New York around 1820, this red and blue checked 2/2 twill blanket is made from very fine singles of worsted.

- 16 EPI x 42 inches wide = 672 threads x 10 yards = 6,720 yards

So 6,720 is the total number of yards of yarn you will need for the warp of your two-panel blanket.

Now take your total number of yards of yarn (6,720) and divide that by the number of yards in 1 pound of Shetland yarn (1,800).

- 6,720 divided by 1,800 = 3.73

So you will need about 3¾ pounds of Shetland yarn for the warp. One quarter of this amount will be in a different color, so you will need 3 pounds of one color and 1 pound of another color. Don't forget that you will also need more of the same yarns for the filling.

Heavyweight Blanket

Materials

- Harrisville Highland Yarn for the warp (900 YPP) in one color
- Harrisville Shetland Yarn for the filling (1,800 YPP) in a different color

Sett and Calculations

The sett is 12 EPI. The length for a three-panel blanket plus a throw is 14 yards. Here are the calculations if you are weaving panels that are 32 inches wide:

- 12 EPI x 32 inches wide = 384 threads x 14 yards = 5,376 total yards of yarn in the warp
- 5,376 yards divided by 900 yards per pound = 5.97, or 6 pounds of warp yarn, of which ¼ will be a different color

Here are the calculations if you are weaving panels that are 42 inches wide:

- 12 EPI x 42 inches wide = 504 x 10 yards = 5,040 total yards of yarn in the warp
- 5,040 divided by 900 yards per pound = 5.6 pounds of warp, of which ¼ will be a different color

You are making a checked blanket that must be seamed in the center, so start the warp with a ½ block. That way, when you seam the blanket together, the two panels will make the same size square at the center.

The color pattern is a square of natural, or another color of your choice, consisting of 24 threads and a stripe of 8 threads of midnight blue, or another color of your choice.

Start your warp with 16 threads of natural, then wind 8 midnight blue, then 32 natural, then 8 midnight blue. Do this nine times and end with 16 threads of natural.

Threading

A reversing draw in the threading allows you to weave a herringbone pattern. There is no need to thread a special selvage on this weave structure.

- Start by threading three straight draws: (1,2,3,4) x 3.
- Then thread three reversing draws, but do not repeat the 4.
- Begin on the 3,2,1,4 and repeat that 3 times.
- Then thread three straight draws as before, but again, do not repeat the 4.
- Begin on the 1,2,3,4. Continue this across the entire warp.

Tying up the Treadles

Use the same system of tie-up for the treadles as for the twill scarf.

- The first outside treadle on the left will be tied to harnesses 1 and 2.
- The outside treadle on the right will be tied to harnesses 2 and 3.
- The inside treadle on the left will be tied to harnesses 3 and 4.
- The inside treadle on the right will be tied to harnesses 1 and 4.

Because you can weave 1/1 plain weave in this threading, if you have two treadles on the inside, you can tie them up to harnesses 1 and 3 and 2 and 4 to weave a 1/1 plain weave.

Tip: Twill weaves have a definite direction in which the very last warp ends may not be caught. If you notice this, switch your shuttle to the other side in the same shed, or reverse the direction that you are weaving your twill. If this doesn't solve the problem, rethread the last four ends of your warp 1,4,2,3. That will catch at least 2 ends every other time, which is quite sufficient.

The Treadling

Treadle and throw in the same manner as in other weaves.

- Step on the left outside treadle and throw from the left hand. Beat and change sheds.
- Step on the outside right treadle, and throw from the right side. Beat and change sheds.
- Step on the treadle second from the outside on the left, and throw left.
- Step on the second treadle from the outside right, and throw right.

Herringbone-Checked Blanket

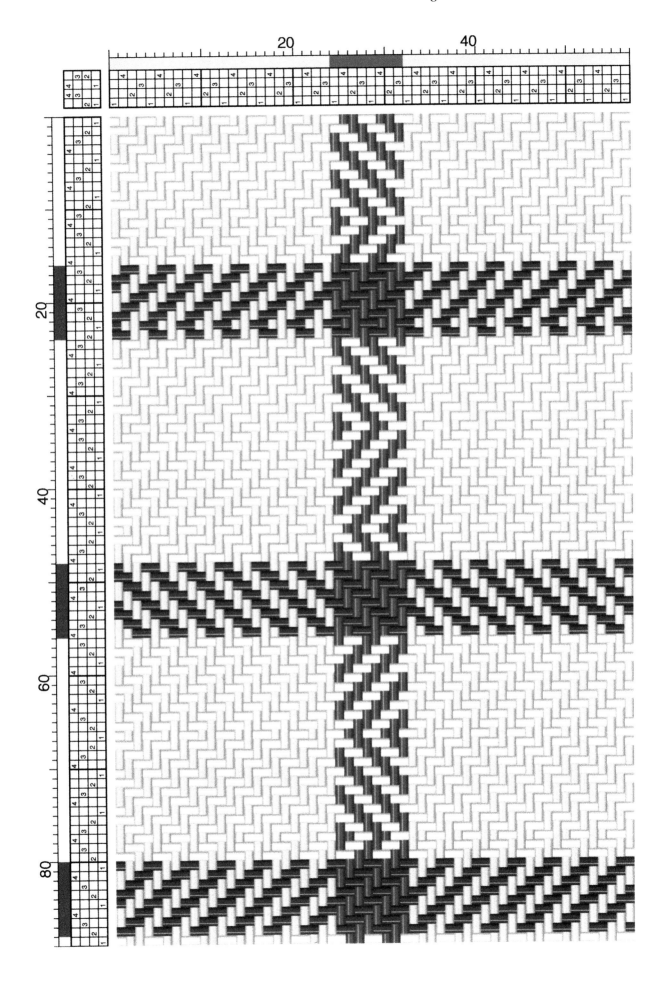

Diamonds Made on the Herringbone Threading

This is a four-pick sequence. Beat so that the diagonal of the twill is at close to a 45-degree angle or greater. Remember that you are not making the blanket the density you want on the loom; you are making a web with about the same number of picks per inch as you have in the warp.

Weave the natural or ground color to an optical square, then change shuttles.

Run a tape measure along the length of the web as you are weaving, and plan for 20 percent shrinkage after finishing. If you want your panel to finish 88 inches long after washing, then you should weave the panel 105 inches long on the loom.

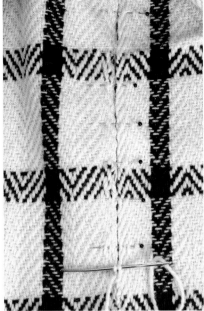

Using a Template

Once you have woven a small sample and feel that your beat is even and that you understand the treadling, count your picks per inch and how many throws make a square of the ground color.

Switch shuttles. Do not cut off the ground shuttle. It will carry up along one side of the panel.

Weave with the stripe color and see whether 8 or fewer throws of the shuttle give you the right size for the checked pattern. Always use an even number of picks so that the color change is always on the same side.

Weave two or three blocks of the pattern, and then cut a piece of cardboard. Lay it on top of your woven pattern for at least two full repeats.

Mark the size of the ground and the check so that you have a template. As you weave, use the template to keep the pattern repeats the same size. This will be useful in matching the two or three panels together.

Creating Diamond Patterns in Twill Weave

You already know that the reversing draw pattern of this threading allows us to weave a herringbone pattern. If you reverse the treadling in the same way that you are reversing the threading, you can create diamonds.

You will still be weaving a 2/2 twill, so the diamonds will be balanced. Both sides of the cloth will look the same. A draft of this diamond pattern is included here as an option for your blanket.

Finishing

After weaving both panels, take the web from the loom and lay it on a flat surface. Cut the panels apart and lay them side-by-side.

It is best to join the panels with a butt seam. Bring the two selvages together and use the same yarn you wove with to sew the two panels together. Whip-stitch them securely, but make sure that the panels remain flat.

Blankets usually have a small, rolled hem and sometimes an additional blanket stitch over the hems. A short fringe is also another way to end a blanket. Once woolen yarn is washed, it will not unravel so no sewing is necessary.

Washing the Blanket

Yarns are spun using spinning oil. This must be removed so that the woolen yarn will get soft.

In your washing machine, fill the tub with lukewarm water. Add at least one full cup of detergent. Use a dye-free, good-quality liquid laundry detergent.

Put the blanket in the machine and make sure it is thoroughly wet. There should not be any dry areas. Agitate it for a few seconds and then *let it soak* for 20 to 30 minutes.

Put the machine on the large setting and the medium wash cycle and start it.

After washing, place the blanket in the dryer on low heat and tumble dry until just barely damp.

If it is not soft enough, repeat the process. The blanket can be washed again and again throughout its life on the cool and gentle settings.

The shrinkage should be 20 percent or less, and since you planned for this, you should have a blanket that is approximately 88 inches long.

PROJECT 4

Cotton and Linen Table Set in Bronson Lace (Tied Spot Weave)

Another weave structure that is historic but lends itself to very creative modern applications is spot weave. Spot weave is based on plain weave, with areas that resemble tic-tac-toe floats used to create a design.

Historic Spot Weave

Made in about 1820, this tablecloth is made of five-harness weave singles linen warp and filling. The face shows the warp floats. The knotted fringe is a plied cotton that was added to the tablecloth. The bottom photo shows the pattern blocks of a table-cloth made with five-harness spot weave.

You can easily recognize spot weave by examining first one surface of the fabric and then the other side. The floats on one surface are *warp floats*, and those on the other surface are *filling floats*. The floats are surrounded by areas of 1/1 plain weave.

In the 1920s, the grand dames of the weaving revival came across this tied spot-weave structure in J. and R. Bronson's book *The Domestic Manufacturer's Assistant*, published in Utica, New York, in 1817. The dames named this spot-weave structure after the authors, calling it "Bronson lace." It was not invented by the Bronsons, and it, in fact, predates them by a hundred years or more, but using the revival version is a great way for handweavers with four harnesses to create beautiful patterns. Most of the true spot-weave designs in the Bronson book and other period weavers' draft books use at least five harnesses.

New in This Project

- Reading a Bronson lace (tied spot weave) draft on four harnesses
- Reading a spot-weave draft for four and five harnesses
- Working with linen yarn
- Working with finer yarns

Materials:

- 1 pound of 20/2 bleached cotton, mercerized or unmercerized (8400 YPP)
- 1 pound of 40/2 wet-spun bleached linen

Sett and Calculations

Make your warp 18 inches wide and the sett 40 EPI for 720 ends.

- 18 inches x 40 EPI = 720

If you decide that you do not want to work in fine yarn you can use a heavier cotton (16/2 or 10/2), adjust the end count down to 36 EPI, and redo the calculations.

Your filling yarn should be the same size as your warp, so if you do want to use a heavier cotton yarn, then you need to use a heavier linen yarn as well. If you choose an unbleached linen, you will also create a nice contrast but the look of the cloth will be different.

A warp that is 6 yards long will yield 8 napkins or a runner and 4 napkins.

- 6 yards x 720 warp ends = 4,320 total yards
- 4,320 total yards of warp divided by 8,400 yards per pound = .51

That means that you will use about a half-pound of 20/2 cotton for the warp.

Threading Draft for Spot Weave and Bronson Lace

Spot weave uses a single harness as a ground. The pattern blocks are made using the other harnesses. You create one block for each harness other than the ground harness, so on a four-harness loom in simple spot weave you would have three pattern blocks.

However, you *cannot* use the same pattern block twice in a row. This problem is eliminated if you take one harness as a tie-down harness. That is what is accomplished in tied spot weave, or Bronson lace.

Bronson lace, tied spot weave on four harnesses, uses one harness for the ground, but then uses a second harness as a tie-down, so that the pattern blocks can be repeated, as in Ms and Os.

The threading of both spot weave and Bronson lace allows you to weave 1/1 plain weave across the warp, as well as weaving the spot patterns. In Ms and Os you could not weave a plain weave across the warp.

Tip: It does not matter which harness is the ground harness, so before you begin, if you have more heddles on one of your harnesses, use that harness as the ground. Write the draft using harness 1 as the ground harness, but that is only a convenience for writing the draft.

Tied Spot-Weave Bronson Lace

Spot Weave on Four Shafts

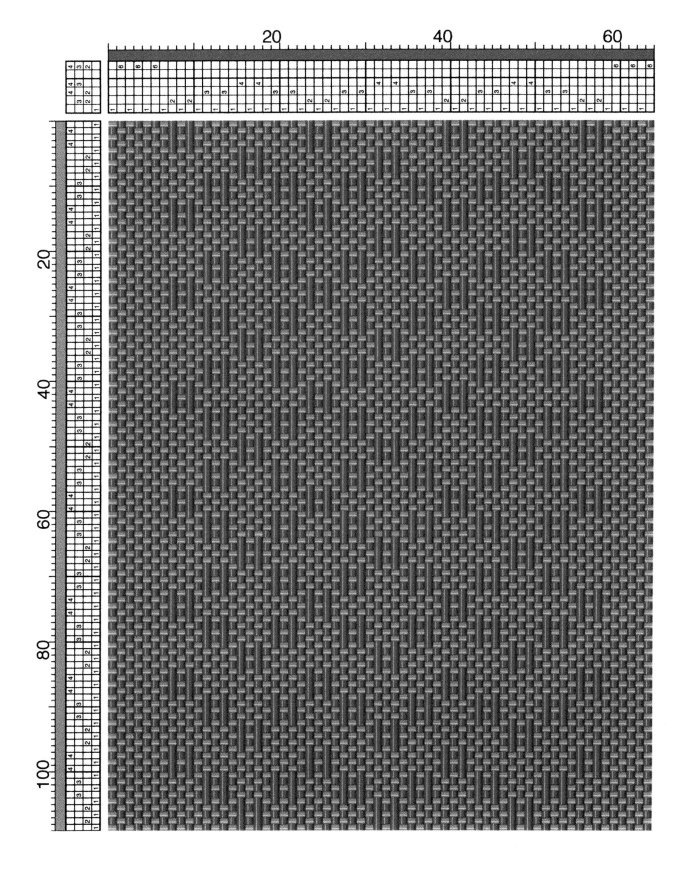

Spot Weave on 5 Shafts

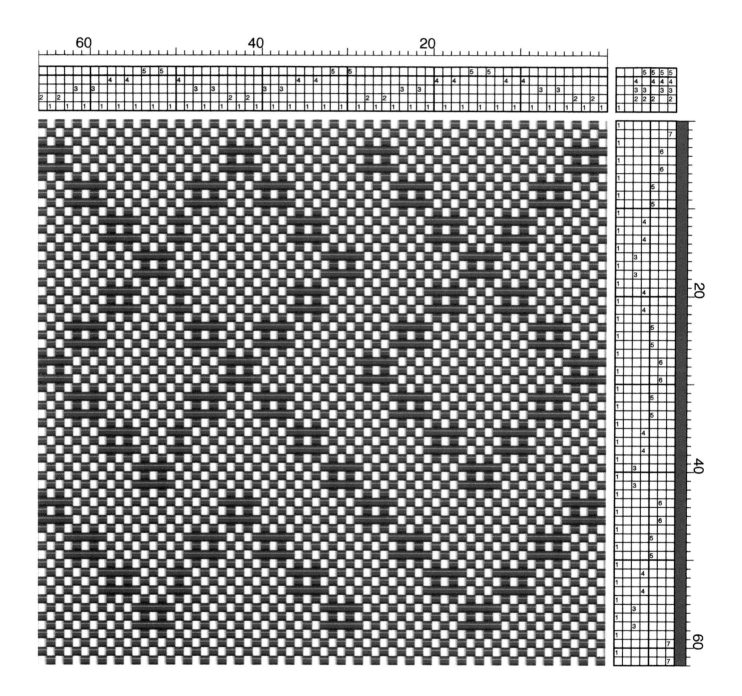

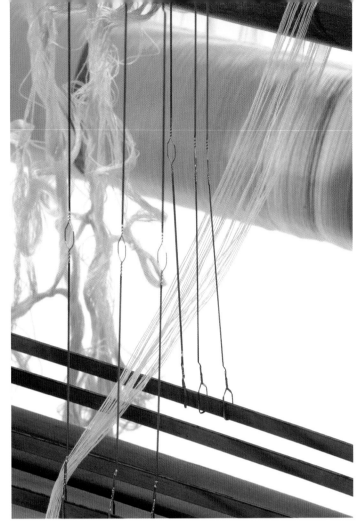

You may need to move heddles from one harness to another so that you have enough heddles to accommodate your pattern. As with the Ms and Os placemats, these napkins should have a border, a center repeat, and then the border repeated on the other side.

Counting off threads before you start entering through your harness is useful because it ensures that the napkin will be balanced and that you will know if you need to move heddles before you start.

If you want an 18-inch napkin, plan your border to be 3 inches on each side. The border consists of 120 ends, or 20 repeats of the 6-thread unit: 1,2,1,2,1,4.

Count 120 threads from the other side of your warp and tie a slip knot. Next count off the little inner border of four repeats of the second unit 1,3,1,3,1,4. That will use 24 threads. Count 24 threads from the other side toward the center as well.

When you have finished threading the border and the inner border, alternate the units until you reach your slip knot on the other side. Then begin threading the inner border and then the border.

Sley whatever combination works for the sett and the reed you have. Remember it is always better to sley more ends in a wider reed than to sley single in a fine reed.

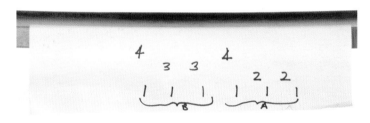

The Treadling

Again, with a one-shuttle weave, set up your treadles so that you will be throwing left when stepping left and throwing right when stepping right.

In tied spot weave this is easy, as every other pick will always be just harness 1 and treadle 1 (if harness 1 is your ground). Adjust your tie-up so that whichever harness is your ground is on the left outside treadle.

Sampling the Weave in Contrasting Colors

As with all the other projects, I recommend that you weave a sample before you start weaving your napkins. For this project, try weaving a sample with a contrasting filling color (an example is on page 103). Use a colored cotton of the same weight as the linen you will use to weave your napkins. (See the yarn comparison chart on page 107.)

Using a contrasting color for your sample will help your eye get used to the pattern you are weaving. This is important because when you are weaving tone-on-tone (white on white, in this case) it is more difficult to proof the pattern. It's important for your eye to see the two different block patterns and to learn which treadle combinations give you each block. This is easier if you are looking at a sample with a warp that is one color and a filling that is another contrasting color.

If you like, you can use your sample to make a table mat or runner. Try a variety of colors when you are weaving your samples.

To Make a 1/1 Plain Weave

Treadle 1 on the left will be tied to harness 1.
The treadle on the right outside will be tied to harnesses 2, 3, and 4.
Harness 1 moves every other thread, and the other harnesses carry all the other ends.
To treadle the pattern, tie the two other right treadles:

- The second from the right: harnesses 2 and 4
- The third from the right: harnesses 3 and 4

The treadling sequence for the first unit follows:

- Harness: 1
- Harnesses: 2 and 4
- Harness: 1
- Harnesses: 2 and 4
- Harness: 1
- Harnesses: 2 and 3 and 4
- Repeat this until the border is a square.

The second unit is treadled as follows:

- Harness: 1
- Harnesses: 3 and 4
- Harness: 1
- Harnesses: 3 and 4
- Harness: 1
- Harnesses: 2 and 3 and 4
- Repeat this until the inner border is square. Then alternate the units for the center of the napkin or runner. When you have the center portion square, begin the inner border and then the large outer border.

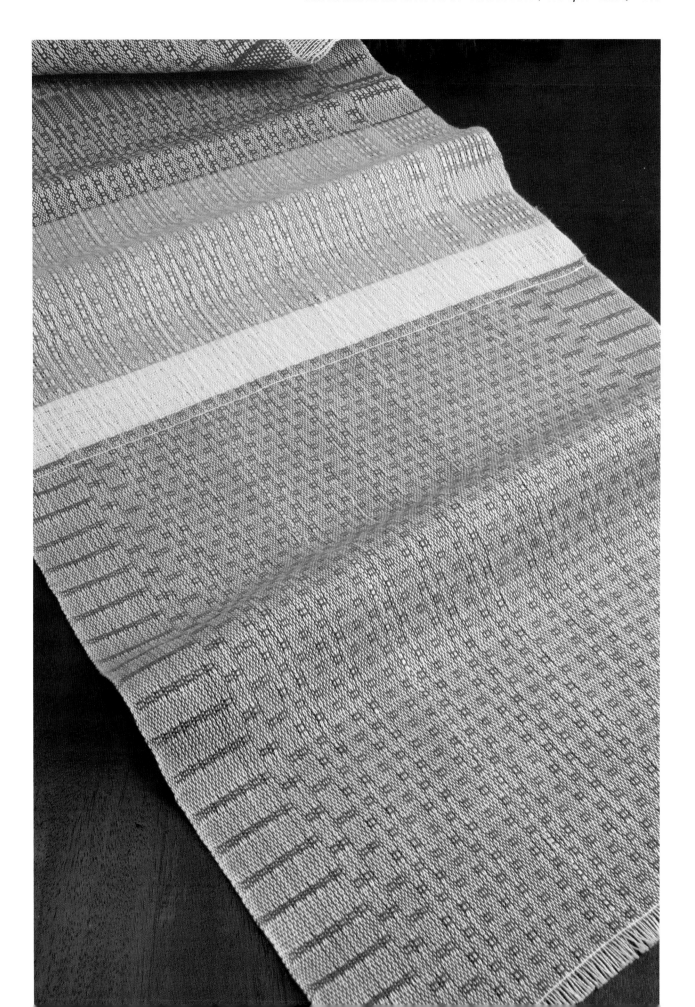

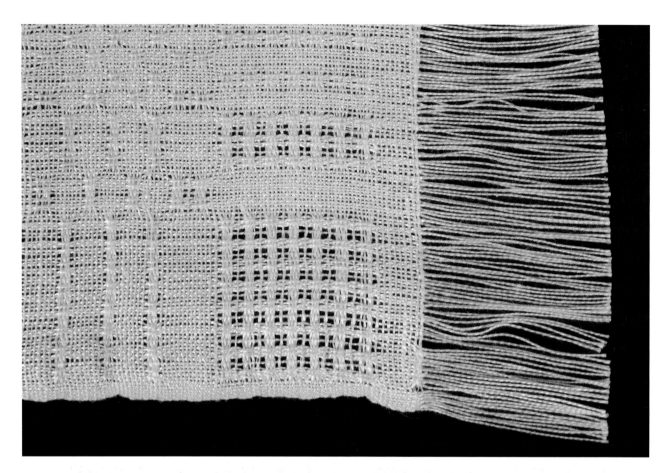

Finishing

After weaving your warp, trim and repair the web. Sew across both cut ends of the web. Fill your washing machine tub with lukewarm water and a little soap. Soak the web in the water for ten minutes and then run it through a rinse and spin cycle (gentle or delicate setting). Put it in the dryer on delicate.

Take the fabric out of the dryer and cut the pieces apart. You can either sew a small hem all the way around each napkin or create a short fringe on the napkin edges by sewing a line of stitching ¼ inch in from the cut edges and removing any loose picks.

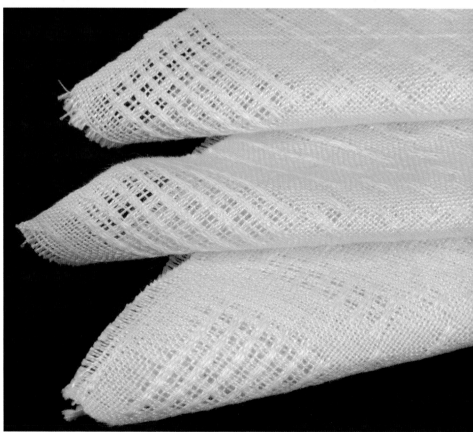

Weaving Float-Work Patterns

Another weave structure that will be helpful to learn is one in which the woven design blocks are repeated in the filling and must be held in place with a second shuttle carrying a ground that holds the repeated filling pick in place. This then becomes a two-shuttle weave with a ground and a pattern shuttle.

The most popular form of this is *float work*, in which the pattern picks float over all of the warp threads in a block using the same shed opening.

In order to repeat a pattern pick without changing the shed, a smaller, finer yarn is thrown across the web in a ground weave, usually plain weave, so that the pattern pick can be repeated. The sequence consists of one pick of a pattern shed and then one pick with a second shuttle in a plain weave shed, usually of shafts 1 and 3 or 2 and 4, using a finer yarn. The ground shuttle "chases" the pattern shuttle and alternates the two sheds of plain weave no matter what pattern shed is being thrown before it. This means that a pattern shuttle is thrown from the left to the right and the filling beaten in place, and then the ground shuttle is thrown also from the left to the right, following the pattern shuttle, but in its own shed of plain weave.

The advantage of this weave structure for the weaver with four shafts is that on four shafts you can produce a four-block pattern with ease. The possibilities of making different patterns with block work become much greater as a result.

Float Work Draft

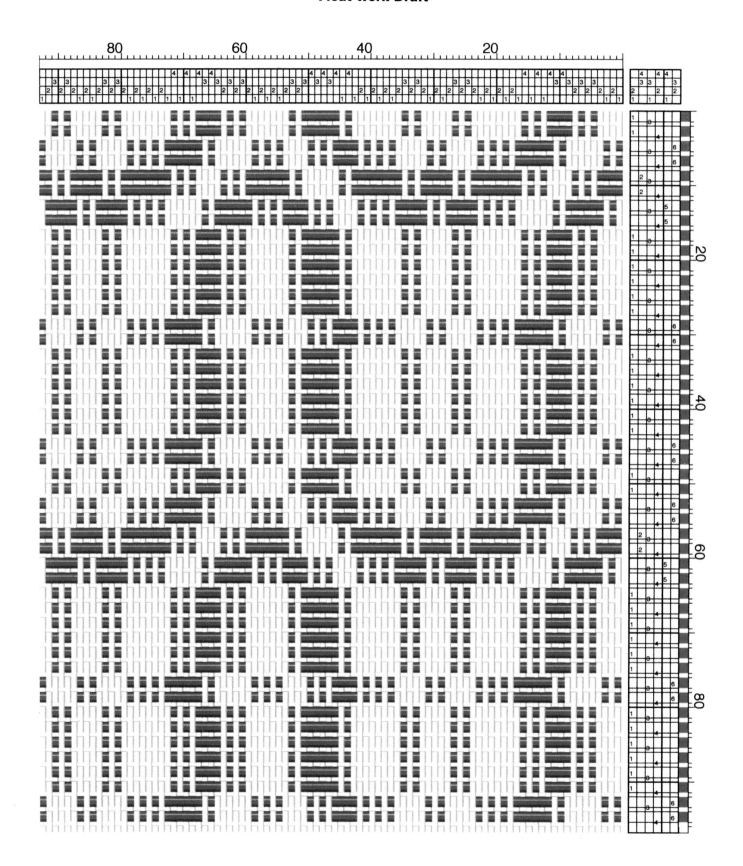